A Conversation With the Sages

Taking the Path That Leads to Love, Happiness, and Success

Sara Ahavah

Copyright © 2020 by Dr Shelah Harris, PhD

All rights reserved. This book or any portion thereof may not be reproduced or used in any manner whatsoever without the express written permission of the publisher except for the use of brief quotations in a book review.

Printed in the United Kingdom

First Printing – February 2021

ISBN 978-1-905803-20-0

Sara Ahavah Publishing

61 Bridge Street, Kington, HR5 3DJ

Table of Contents

About the author   5

Acknowledgement   7

Introduction   10

1. What is the purpose of my life?   24

2. Is there such a thing called fate, which dictates the cause of my life?   42

3. What stops me from evolving into my greater self?   54

4. Why is it that I cannot feel truly happy?   70

5. What can be done to improve my relationships with others?   84

6. Why do bad things happen to good people and vice versa?   98

7. What is love?   116

8. Author's conclusion and action points   132

Other Resources   152

About the author

Sara Ahavah (pen name of Dr Shelah Harris) is a spiritual counsellor, teacher, and author of self-help personal development books designed to support readers broaden their horizons for positive change in their lives. Her career started as a chartered certified accountant but did not stop there with her keen interest in spirituality.

In the decade leading to her intensive spiritual studies, Sara worked tirelessly supporting voluntary organisations in the United Kingdom. She played various roles as a non-executive director, chair of the board of governors, chair of finance and standard sub-committees, as well as a treasurer for several organisations. In 2012, in her quest for more answers to her dilemmas and challenges, she gave up all appointments to devote her time to spiritual education.

Over the last fifteen years, she has dedicated her life to researching and studying spiritual laws for personal development and growth to resolve numerous life challenges and heal emotional traumas.

In 2018, Sara became a Philosopher of Metaphysical Sciences, PhD, and with this began assisting others to learn new skills to redefine their life's purpose, build healthy and loving relationships, and master self-help tools to recover from emotional hurts. This book has been written to empower the reader to shift their paradigm about life and its purpose as well as take the path that leads to happiness, success, joy, and love as shared in its various chapters.

To find out more about the author, visit her website www.sarainnerhealing.com

Twitter – https://twitter.com/wisdom_sages

Facebook Page – The Sages Wisdom

Facebook Group – The Sages Wisdom

YouTube – The Sages Wisdom

Instagram – Dr Shelah Harris

Acknowledgement

As I reflected on this book's contents, I concluded that every experience in my life was designed to bring personal spiritual development and growth of one sort or another. I never expected my perception of life would be so transformed, leading me to a point where the good, the bad, and the ugly are accepted as my soul's gifts. Life is full of mysteries that everyone, in their own time, will uncover in their journey towards the purpose of their existence. It is genuinely so.

I remembered so well how I searched for the meaning of life in all different directions, often being left more in the dark than before my search. Every step of the way, I have met teachers who, in many ways, brought me to my final destination, where I would begin to make sense of my life, my world, my purpose, and what happens next. Even though I may not understand it all, I want to thank them all; they are many to refer to by name.

My children had always been my motivation to find out more about life. I never wanted them to suffer or experience the dark side of life as I did. I wished the best for them, but I could not give them what I truly believe they deserve. In my desperation to make the best of my life, they have genuinely been the impetus for my change journey, though they may not entirely be aware of this. Therefore, I want to thank them and, most importantly, my son, who inspired me to take on my writing project when I nearly gave it up.

My parents are also significant to me. My mum passed on in 2013 at a time I was beset with many challenges. In truth, she is in my heart, and I do not feel detached from her. I feel obliged to thank my parents for the part they played in my life. My mother taught me at a very early age to pray. She ensured I learned many of the psalms, which became the inner guide in times of trouble. My dad taught me a good work ethic. These two qualities have been assets that I will never change. Through their struggles, I learnt the art of forgiveness and became desperate to search for truth that will make a difference. They helped me find my purpose to break the cycle of the past and empower the future generation. They helped me to break the mentality that so often leads me in the path of suffering through conflicts. I became sick of being sick from dysfunctional patterns.

I have many friends who helped me edit this book that I wish to thank. Their support inspired me to move forward. The ultimate thanks go to my spiritual teacher, who made it possible to have conversations with the sages over the last six years.

Through the conversations, I began to see how every event has been a silent message knocking at the door of my heart to break the mentality that held me bound in the web of unhappiness. To stop blaming others and put myself in the driving seat with the key of my life to move towards the ultimate goal of unity, love, connection and harmony. No matter what happens in my life, the gift these conversations have given is priceless. Money can never buy peace, and I gained inner peace, harmony, happiness, and joy through these conversations.

With this in mind, this book is dedicated to the sages who have gone before and those who are with us today. They are the true spiritual masters that have been the channel for enlightenment into our world. All the sacred books we treasure today came forth through them. Therefore, all credit goes to them.

Introduction

Suppose you are invited for a private session with several mighty sages; as you sit down in their office, you are greeted with a smile and gently asked what questions you require answers to in order to help you live a better life on this planet – what would you ask?

Sure enough, you will have your own questions; you may want to ponder on them. What would be your top seven questions for the sages? In this book, seven of the most frequently life challenging questions based on research studies are answered. Incidentally, these were the seven questions I needed to be answered during my conversations with the sages.

When I look back at my life and the journey I had to travel before my conversations with the sages, I cannot help asking why I was so blinded to the solutions for all my predicaments, why I could not see the master key that opens the doors to love, happiness and success even though it was right in front of me. I cannot ask why I chose the path of self-love despite experiencing the futility and suffering that comes with it, why I could not see the inevitable failure that awaits my goal to attain happiness, love, and success if I am unwilling to align with nature's law of love thy neighbour as thyself.

My conversations with the sages have been life-changing. They have marked the beginning of a new era that compelled me to re-engineer a new way of living. They have shifted my paradigm of the world I live in, and they provided a new way of perceiving life and raising consciousness. No longer would I seek materialism over the importance of healthy connection, which in itself is mind-blowing for someone so self-centred, independent, and who frequently devalued the power of connection with others.

Every conversation with the sages was a jaw-dropping experience, leaving me with one conclusion: we as humans are interconnected. At the core of our being, we share similar sensations, which inevitably lead us to ask similar questions about life. By the time you hit the age of forty, I doubt you will not be asking many of the questions dealt with in this book. By the time you hit fifty, your childhood fantasies about life will have been challenged many times over just as mine were, which led me to find solutions where I least expected.

I remember how I prepared myself for these conversations. I have concluded that humans are bedevilled with questions for the most part of our lives when faced with challenges and struggles for which no end is at hand. I have asked many times, Why are we so challenged? What is going on? We need answers, and we needed them yesterday, yet we cannot find the correct solutions to heal our pain, whether spiritual, physical, mental, or emotional. Why is this happening to us?

You may have been down this path as many of my friends and families confessed; they have silently asked similar questions. If only I had met the sages sooner, life could have been different. However, I am grateful that no matter what my experiences have been, these conversations took place before I turned fifty.

I am grateful; I still have the opportunity to share some of these conversations with my children. My son, in particular, has been privy to most of my new findings of life. I love my kids dearly and wanted them to understand how life works, navigate the journey to happiness and success, and avoid the pitfalls of mistakes made by parents and older adults in their lives.

Parents are put in the unenviable position of demonstrating a good model to their kids who cannot understand why they fail to perform well. I remembered blaming my parents, until I hit the same position where I failed to live the standards expected and disappointed my kids. I am grateful that even my great-grandchildren will benefit from this book, and I hope you as a reader and your family will gain the life-transforming benefit it offered me. This is the reason I was inspired to share it with you. Had I not been armed with the knowledge and experience gained through these sages, an experience I had at a university last year, which I will share later, would have been missed. I would have continued deluding myself that all a person needs for success, love, and happiness are academic qualifications. I would have paid minute attention to the gems offered by the sages and remained frustrated, hurtful, and unhappy. Let me now share with you that university experience.

Nature has a way of sending us messages through different challenges, although we are sometimes so busy with mundane activities – we miss them. So busy we can sometimes be, the solutions to our problems are handed to us, but we have ears that cannot hear, and eyes that cannot see. After many conversations with the sages, nature set me up with new events that put me on the spot and tested how serious I am about taking the path that leads to love, happiness, and success.

I was invited to attend a graduation ceremony when I had many challenges with my ex-husband. There were many obstacles to overcome with this event and many battles to win in mind. I had to attend this event alongside my ex-husband, and we were certainly not on friendly terms. We have been divorced for a while, but there was much unfinished business to deal with, matters which were bitter and cruel and with serious financial consequences. I was stretched financially over legal fees and costs and attending the event alongside him was another financial pressure I had to deal with. I never expected matters between us would turn out the way they were unfolding with no end in sight. My first hurdle to overcome was finances to get to the event. Next was ensuring all family members felt comfortable and happy on the day without any upset that would spoil the event. I recall many temptations to back off. I had good reason to do so. Why should I spend time next to a man who had caused me so much pain? Had I not suffered enough? The thoughts kept screaming through my mind. I must confess I struggled big time. The conversation with the sages saved my life to move forward with this matter, but it was not without many inner battles.

I recall how I read through my notes taken during my conversations with the sages, hoping to find answers that would see me escaping the event with a well-justified statement. But alas, this was never going to be a quick escape. Turning the pages of my notes, one of the messages screamed out at me: 'Love covers all transgression'. As I read through the notes, I remember responding, 'Yeah, but this is too deep a transgression; sure enough, I have forgiven him, but I will not sit through an entire ceremony with him'. I continued reading my notes, and another message jumped out at me. It was simple: 'What will your action say about your commitment to connect and build relationships with others?' Would you prefer to continue to hold past events in your mind and deny yourself the wonderful opportunities to set a good example for others who depend on you? What good are the conversations with the sages if you are not prepared to follow them? By this time, my mind was saturated with debates between a 'for' and an 'against' camp.

I was astonished that no matter the nature of wisdom one gains through their education, the process of implementation is never easy. One must conquer their ancient mindset to allow the new wisdom to take root. This was my opportunity to dig out the weeds of the past and sow the seeds for future harvest. The choice is mine. Whatsoever you do today will determine the nature of the fruits you harvest in the future. The big question for me was this: 'What will you sow this year and what harvest do you expect in the future?' These thoughts raced through my mind, and I was still nowhere near deciding. It took me another week or two before I plucked up the courage to ask for help from the Creator (Nature) to assist. Nature is the force that governs our universe. It is not a person. The sages have told us it is omnipresent, omnipotent and omniscient. Everything is operated by Nature. Our hearts and all other organs in the human body are controlled by Nature. The same applies to all the animals, the plants, the minerals and even those beings we know nothing about at this stage. We call Nature by many names – Creator, God, Universal Intelligence and more.

Everyone has to walk through the path of giving love to others they feel do not deserve it. You have received love when you did not deserve it. Now is the time for you to give it and subsequently, you will have many more opportunities to do so. The thoughts continued racing in my mind. I was left thinking, the path to happiness is a high and tall order. One needs to thread above the familiar old mindset, which is painful, particularly with the uncertainties of the future yields from the new mindset. One has to give up the old ways for the new ways, totally trusting that the sages' wisdom will prove beneficial down the line. One has to give love and happiness to others with no expectation of receiving.

In silence, I settled that I would take the path to love and attend the event, covering the offences with love for all the family members' benefit. I would do so as an act of love for the family members whose happiness was more important than mine. And with this decision made in my mind, the matter was settled, and the family members were informed.

While sitting at the graduation ceremony, nothing prepared me for what I was about to hear next. The university's dean gave his speech, which was watched and listened to by thousands of people on that fine summer day. I listened with alertness at every word he uttered. He was a well-educated man with an eloquence that captivated his audience – a rare specialism for the role he played that day. I had always believed that universities were the dispensary of all the knowledge graduates will need to travel life's journey successfully. His closing statement left me speechless. The dean confessed openly that the university had done its best to instil skills required for economic success. That was why the students signed up to study at the university, and the job was done. Every student had qualified to go out into the world to become a professional in their particular fields. What he said next was profound. He made it clear that the qualifications by themselves did not guarantee that all the students would succeed in life. He urged all the students to be nice to people, to be kind to one another if they genuinely wanted to be successful.

I remember asking in the serenity of my mind – why were these students not told the university does not guarantee personal success as part of their services before they paid their fees and committed to the program? Of course, no one studies the subject of kindness as a curriculum in schools or universities. I pondered a rather disturbing message I have received and wondered if the students understood his message's depth. I left that day wondering why someone would incur loans of £40,000 or more to learn a profession that does not guarantee success. I was baffled that the core essential ingredients for success were missing from the curriculum – was this deliberate? Did the university expect students to have learned these core skills at home or previous schools? Is this how Nature organises the system for human development? And if so, what happens to those whose home life did not instil these qualities prior to university? Is that also part of Nature's grand plan? Should the university be tolerated in continuing to provide half an education at the expense of the students? My thoughts were racing and endless.

I reflected on my own life and those of many who are intellectually educated. I concluded the dean was correct. Many of the intellectually educated people I know are far from being happy. I suspect they, too, would not have known kindness was an essential ingredient for success. Academic qualifications are not a ticket to success. I can attest to this, given my own experiences that have left me challenged and those of my older relatives and friends.

When I took the path of higher academic education, I thought it would deliver all the knowledge for success and was convinced that was all I needed as an avid learner. I put so much faith in my education; I thought my next milestone was to find a husband and start building my next conquest. Sure enough, I hit the next milestones and violated all the rules of nature to get there. Does this sound familiar? What was life for you as a youngster growing up? Did you have goals and visions to accomplish and conquer the world? Maybe you did or not; whatever camp you found yourself in, life as a journey compels us to evolve and grow.

I had my children shortly after I graduated. With confidence, I groomed them for university. Ignorant of the shortfall in mainstream education, as well as my own capacity to instil the essential ingredients for success, they were handed my ancient mindset devoid of kindness, true love, empathy, good relationships and harmony. But something hit home to me. I was now with qualifications, a family, and a well-paid job struggling big time with relationships. Happiness was far from me. Everything I thought was under my control was proving to be the opposite. Nature did not have it my way. If only I had met the sages earlier, they might have guided me. One by one, I began to feel disappointment, pain, and regret. I began to feel resentment and anger. A well-paid job cannot buy true love, happiness, and peace. Where could I now turn to get my frustration fixed? Everyone's path is different. Your frustrations might have been over health issues or the loss of a love one, the loss of a sense of dignity, security, confidence and more. Whatever the experience, we often feel similar negative emotions that shift our perspective and send us off towards the journey to search for the meaning of life.

My questioning of the validity of the education I have obtained began to haunt me well into my forties. I wanted to be successful, yet I was faced with so many pitfalls that were never covered in my education. I was desperate, and I began searching for answers. By this time, my kids had been brainwashed to believe higher education was their ticket to success, as well as in the importance of the Christian faith. Needless to say, I did not even understand the depth and true meaning of the teachings of Jesus. I remembered it so well, the day I questioned what is the Kingdom of Heaven and the importance of 'Love Thy Neighbour As Thyself'? I can no longer stand for clichés I do not really live on a daily basis. This resulted in me turning every knowledge I held as truth on its head. When one knows the truth they are set free. I have spoken with many people in my lifetime. I have listened to many life-changing events. The stories are different. The experiences are different. What is similar is the sense of frustration, anger and loss that people are left with when challenged. That is what connects the human spirit and will continue to bring us closer to each other.

My conversations with the sages taught me how limited our education is. The breadth of skills and qualities required for success are often underplayed until one begins to meet with failure and disappointment. The link between our thought life, mental processes, emotions, and spirit are often unknown, yet they play a significant part in our progress. The societal moral excellence and the art of healthy relationship building may well be relegated as unimportant. Until we find ourselves unable to build harmonious relationships to succeed in all spheres of our lives, a shift in our paradigm is remote. Why is the fabric for success excluded from our primary and secondary education? What good is the academic if the spiritual qualities needed for success are not developed in a person?

I hastened to conclude that an education devoid of spiritual essence is like a man without a soul that makes him no different from the animals. Everyone wants to be happy. Give a person all the luxury in the world without feeding the soul part of his life; it will take a few months, if not hours, for him to realise emptiness. Happiness and joy are what we seek at the highest level. Yet, they are not gifts we can obtain over the counter with money as they are the real wealth that we strive for, though unconsciously. They are fruits derived from the higher plane, which of course, are treasured by the human race, which has a profound tendency to reject the investment needed to reap the desired harvest. Peace and harmony are similarly treasured gifts, but yet their causal and effective relationship is seldom understood. Moreover, we very rarely appreciate that nature will not hand us fruits for seeds we did not plant. Sooner or later, everyone will realise that a holistic investment is needed to attain love, happiness, and success.

The dean was correct: it is impossible to dispute that kindness and love are not essential qualities for success; they are. How unfortunate for those who have still not been awakened to this realisation. As my mind raced, I thought about the importance of calming down and being present for the students whose accomplishments were being celebrated. I wished success for them but knew they would need to play their part in the system to earn it. The ceremony concluded. All the niceties and courtesies were expressed between family members. I had received a great lesson and confirmation that my precious notes during my conversations with the sages were priceless. I wish I could share them with the dean of the university – I wondered if he would accept the wisdom. Never mind, I told myself; perhaps one day this book will find its way to all the universities and students who need to understand life is much more than job skills. The ultimate goal of life is love, happiness, and success. Academic qualifications are valuable but not the passport for happiness and love.

On my way home, I had time enough on board the train to do more reflection. This event took me back to the day I graduated. It was a special day, and I was looking forward to the event. Nothing prepared me for what was to come. That day was mired with chaos as my own parents could not put their discord aside to support me at my graduation. I never realised the significance of their indifference, as I have grown to accept it as the norm. Deep down, I wanted both of them to be there for me. I wanted them to demonstrate love and kindness to each other and myself. However, it was not possible. They were both in their own worlds, and I had to settle for the products of their indifference.

I recall how tense and embarrassed I was at the graduation, and I could barely remember what was said to us on that day. The experience was not the one I would have hoped for; however, I accepted my fate that day. I wondered if my graduation ceremony was anything like the one I had just witnessed. I reflected if similar advice was given to us on that day, but I just could not process it at the time. It was obvious that I have many questions to ask. I have many problems to find solutions to and if the Creator of the universe were present physically that day, I would have asked him these questions as I was burdened.

I struggled to find out why people would spend years in the universities and many other fields of academia, focusing on building success without harmony and connection with others. I wondered why people progress to the broader world to work in a profession until they discover that their education is not sufficient for them to operate efficiently in life. Well, something along those lines. Love, kindness, joy and peace are fruits of our spirit that connect the human race with Nature. Why is the spiritual education side of one's life neglected until we are met with severe failure? If our education system is aware of the root of its failures, why would it not prepare students holistically for success? Something for you to ponder.

For someone to be expected to learn kindness, moral excellence, and love at the age of forty, usually after failing many times due to ignorance, does not seem right to me. To hide the truth from students – that all their efforts to build a career with a qualification from university will be meaningless if they do not develop the added spiritual soft skills – struck me as a bad deal for those who have handed over their hard cash to the university, thinking the opposite.

I concluded the problem with our education system in both developed and developing countries is that only 20 to 30 per cent of what is needed for success in life is taught to students.

The remaining knowledge and skills must be provided by parents, many of whom are in kindergarten on the subject. If parents are ill-prepared to provide the needed spiritual education, many grown-ups and children will learn through challenges in life, and I was one of the products of this generation. We think we know the world we live in and how to operate within it to build success; life's challenges teach us how much we do not know. Life's challenges teach us how much we are to depend on each other to find a solution that works for our betterment.

This book is written for those seeking a concise answer to life's challenging questions about:

- The purpose of life
- The path to happiness and peace
- How to avoid failed relationships
- The path to love and success

As I pondered on the answers to the questions, I could not help but conclude that this book has helped me free others that I have held in emotional bondage of unforgiveness for years.

I trust you will be inspired and empowered to take the courageous steps to do the same as you digest the materials. This process has helped me become more aware of my inner inclinations to disconnect and harm others in thoughts through harsh judgment and actions. My egoistic nature, which stands in the way of love and happiness is without a shadow of doubt on the radar. A person should learn how much they love themselves more than others. Otherwise they are ill-prepared to give up selfishness for good connection. The concepts and wisdom motivated me to take my soul's direction more seriously as part of my personal growth. I never expected to become calmer relative to my previous disposition. As I digested the contents relating to my life's purpose, I have cultivated a sense of purpose that is way beyond my immediate self-centred vision. I wish for you to gain the same benefits or more. Read on and ponder over the responses using the journal section of each chapter.

If you need any further information or wish to be part of a community to discuss this book, you are welcome to join The Sages Wisdom Facebook Group as well as a free course where I provide more details about the concepts.

Chapter 1
What is the purpose of my life?

The sages say, 'We as people grow up learning lots of academic subjects – maths, English, science, history, and so forth. However, we barely know who we are, how we are supposed to interact in our environment, how we are supposed to relate to life's events, our friends, colleagues, spouse, and children for our betterment and the planet as a whole'. For the best part of our lives, we study numerous subjects with expectations of attaining the best of life through our careers. We are baffled when we find emptiness in our inner state instead of what we were genuinely seeking through careers and many material and human pleasures – love, happiness, success, and good health.

At the heart of all we seek, seldom do we actively study and learn from Nature, which in truth is the source of life that holds the answers that we are looking for. We disregard Nature, attempting to impose our self-seeking egoistic laws upon it, and of course, things do not work out the way we want them to. As if this is not bad enough, we go off blaming others for our failures because we think our laws should work. If they do not work, it is because someone else is not complying or sabotaging us. All of these fantasies take place in our mind's solace, and as a self-centred egoist, we believe them to be true.

The simple reality is this: neither you nor I will ever find happiness, love, good health, and true wealth from careers devoid of the essence of Nature. This is a problem, which humanity as a race must resolve as part of the purpose of life. This problem will never be resolved without the awareness of our ego consciousness, which dominates our thoughts, beliefs, actions and emotions. The ego is the force that dictates we are superior to others, we are here to be served by others and we must be rich and famous at the expense of others including our environment. The ego ensures everything we see by default is negative when it does not serve us and positive when it does. This wonderful machinery will have to be the stepping stone for you and all humanity to constrain in order to build a sustainable foundation for success, love, happiness and harmony.

We must know that our careers are the skills and technical know-how we must learn to offer services and products, in exchange for money. This is part of the human egoistic experience. If we do not treat others with kindness, dignity, and justice, we will soon find Mother Nature frowning upon our attitude and, like a strict parent, bringing us in alignment.

We need to ask nature what the purpose of our lives is because it governs and develops our lives. We call nature by different names – God, the Creator, Universal Intelligence, Source, the seventy-two names of God, and many more names. When we ask nature, we will find that the answer is simple – we live to attain the source of life.

Here comes another big question. How do we attain the source of life? This is technically a different question. How do we attain the feeling of the source of life from where life emerges and developed into this world? It is from this point that the very question was imprinted – what is the purpose of life? As humans, we feel this question, but the still, vegetative, and animate creations do not ask what the purpose of their life is? They simply cooperate with nature.

We as humans always think we live to fulfil our desires, which can never be satisfied. Why? The law of growth sees to it that as soon as one desire is satisfied, another evolves. It is no secret that we also think we live to receive without fulfilling others' desires. This mentality is the curse, which on many occasions leaves us wanting and in strife with others. If you observe your thought patterns you will see how your automatic default thinking is about yourself and no one else. The average person thinks about themselves all day long. No matter what they are doing or saying, the thought is always directed towards their personal interest.

Despite our habits of thinking of self at the expense of others, we can never be satisfied with our lots if we do not seek to make others happy by fulfilling their desires. Nature teaches this to humanity in silence. Watch the animate and vegetative ecosystem and study it closely – you will see that nothing exists for itself and all cooperate with Nature; hence no branch is foolish enough to start a fight with another and create conflict.

We see people depending on the measure of their life's development from generation to generation, hit a point when the question will be asked – this is not accidental. It is engraved in the source of life itself. Nothing can make a person happy or be fulfilled if he/she does not discover the essence of life, which is the purpose of life. Therefore, your question is no accident. Everyone in the human race will come to the point when the question will be asked.

> *"The force that develops us is in itself the purpose of life."*

The force that develops us is in itself the purpose of life. Therefore, we are to pay close attention to this force. Only when we attain the quality of the force that develops us can we understand the reason for life and why we are living. We attain eternal, complete, whole, and perfect life when we are fully in alignment with the source and essence of life. This is why we were created.

Without knowing why we are living or what we live for, life is not worth living. It is the reason people turn to drugs and sex of all sorts when they cannot find answers to this question. It is the reason people become depressed, frustrated, suicidal, resentful and sad without the answers to this question. A person is incapable of living without clarity on the purpose of life. Only when we discover the force of life – the force that develops us – would we know what we were created for and what is the purpose of our life.

In attaining the source of life, we attain eternal, complete, whole, and perfect lives. At this point, we understand that life is not what we feel now, but rather something much more. Our lives as they are, for the most part, bear no resemblance to the essence and the source of life. The emptiness we feel invokes the question to begin the awakening process, which shifts us internally towards the source of life.

"The emptiness we feel invokes the question – what is the purpose of life?"

To conclude, we live to attain the qualities and actions similar to the source of life we call Nature or God. This source of life is a quality of unconditional love – **the force of giving to everyone.** Unconditional love is self-less and with a strong desire to fulfil the needs of others. It seeks for the whole and not for the self. If you look at the entire ecosystem, you will see that everything in Nature seamlessly work in harmony aside the human race. The sun gives off energy to the rest of the system and with that, the plants produce food for the system and so forth. Nothing is wasted. But there is a problem – the human race. Our egos are the opposite quality to unconditional love. The ego sets us apart from Nature itself. It is a negative force compared to unconditional love, which is a positive energy force. Unlike the source of life, our egos' predominant nature is self-love, which means we distrust others, we expect no favours from others generally aside our closed network, we rarely feel others' needs and we are entirely into our own needs and no more. We are conscious of what makes us happy, and self-love is our quality in reality. As a result, we are different in quality when compared to the source of life.

Here is the secret: although we are very unconscious of this, nature governs us as though we are conscious about this as we are all expected to become like it. We cannot attain wholeness, happiness, and perfection while operating exclusively in self-love, which is the opposite quality of nature and life itself. What we truly need in our lives will only come when we embark on the journey to develop our capacity to become like the source of life. Only at this point will life make sense to us and the question will no longer be asked as the answer will have been realised.

Sara's Reflection

The response to this question has left me internally shaken. I immediately wondered what life would be like if everyone worked in harmony and in the best interest of others. I wondered, why we suffer emotionally, mentally, spiritually and physically. Every event that has left us distressed was due to a perceived loss. If love was our predominant consciousness, I am certain the loss would not have been experienced as an overwhelming event. The abundance of love would have drowned out the weight of any psychological egoistic loss leaving us vibrant and happy.

Throughout my life, I have never been clear about the purpose of my existence. I looked around for many years wondering why people are put on a planet to go through a repeated cycle of events and then pass on as though we are simply a machine operated upon. For me, life became extremely challenging in my forties, and I can remember the day I sat down alone on 1 January 2009 in tears, asking for answers to my prayers. By this time, I had given up handing God a long list of my desires, all of which was driven by my desire for money. Money was not my concern anymore. My security was the focus of my concerns. I felt very insecure and in a dark place. I would have happily handed over my bank balance in exchange for truth. 'God, please release the truth to me' – this was a simple prayer from the depth of my heart. I cannot continue living this way – please help – this was my second prayer. My life made no sense. I had a home, but I was miserable living there. I had a family, but they felt like strangers to me, as they did not understand my desires. I had a career as a chartered certified accountant, but I was not fulfilled by it. I had enough money to live comfortably, but I still felt empty. I was healthy but yet felt plagued. I had a marriage, but it felt like hell on earth, and I did not know what had happened. Nothing made sense anymore. I wanted the veil of truth opened, and in 2010, the answer came in the form of a DVD gift by the title *What the Bleep Do We Know*. From that point onwards, the trajectory of my life brought me to the conversations with sages.

Your own life story will be different from mine. However, we are all on the same spiritual journey. You will have experienced life as highs and lows, hopefully with more highs than lows. Either way, the lows could have been lessened with a significant proportion of the human race operating by the law of loving others unconditionally. Love would have been the balm for every trial and tribulation. As you give love to others in the system, love would have been poured into your own life to heal your challenges in life.

> **"Everyone wants to be loved unconditionally but rarely wants to give the same type of love."**

Love has always been a mystery in my life. I was not awarded a home where love was practised as a child. My childhood experiences were painfully endowed with strife and hurt. As I grew up, my escape route was the Church. For some reason, I felt that the answers to my problems could be found in the Bible. It was as though nature was steering me to the doors of heaven, but I had no keys to open the doors. I knew I had to love, but I did not know how, and with that ignorance, my life took a challenging turn as I grew up. Ego as the predominant consciousness is disconnected from others and self-centred. Until one learns how to work above the ego to connect healthily with others, their support network will be thin and with that no power to rise above the challenges easily.

As I pondered my conversation with the sages, it has been one of the greatest gifts handed to me as a child from an impoverished spiritually educated home. The truth is, most of us are from a similar background. One can be in earthly riches and yet in spiritual poverty concurrently. Poverty in this case, means the inability to understand the true self as a spiritual being, as well as to work above the ego self-centredness to take on the quality of unconditional love. It is easy to say one is loving to others. The ultimate test of love is when one is faced with life challenges. In fact, it is as though Nature stands behind all the challenges to test our ability to focus beyond ourselves to maintain healthy connections with others.

> **"Poverty is the inability to know ones true nature. A community is poor when they operate outside the law of love."**

I remember it so well when I came in contact with this information. I wrote it down in my notebook; and went to bed with the book glued to me. I would wake up reading the responses repeatedly, trying to feel like the source of life. What does it really feel like to be the source of life? I wondered. Supposed everything around me was dead. What does it mean to be dead? I asked myself. I felt something piercing through me. I got it. When we are at a distance from each other we are dead. We do not feel each other. That is truly what it means to be dead. Someone can be walking and consider themselves alive but yet dead spiritually because they have no connection to others. They have no real feelings for others. The dead have no feelings of another person. They simply exist. Sad and scared about the prospect of being considered a human being that walks, speaks and interacts with others in the delusion that I am really alive, I determined it was time to do something different.

If we cannot feel each other's desires as ours, we are all dead people walking around behaving like we are alive. We are dead spiritually until we can feel our connection, which brings us to the quality of the source of life. I got it. It is time to feel like the source of life. To feel this, I must become the source of life. The force that connects all the dead together as one single unit is the source of life. Life is a force that gives and makes all the others feel true connection. It frees us from the illusion of separateness. It frees us from the deception of differences. It unites us to the essence of the source of life.

My notes from the conversations with the sages became a precious diamond; I could not let go of it. No matter what we experience, there is a bigger plan for you and me. Nature puts us through a journey devoid of love for the best part of our lives for specific reasons. You may have been someone who had a loving parental and family environment as a child growing up, which means your experiences are different from mine. Your challenge would not have been the deprivation of parental unconditional love but rather something else. Pause and think about this. Can you understand that everyone has their own life event to deal with and without any exception? Even the king and queens in palaces have their own challenges to deal with. Your challenge will come in the form of many negative events through the lens of your self-centred ego. It might be a disastrous loss of a loved one, a health threat or financial threat and much more. The challenges are there for a purpose. They are intended to test our attitude towards Nature and those around us. Will you continue to be dead by playing the ego selfish game? Would you rather play the game of giving life to all those in your contact?

> **"This is the real choice of our life's purpose – love others as you love yourself."**

This is the game of life. We fall for the ego's spell 99 per cent of the time and continue to remain dead to our spiritual self. Until we become conscious of our spiritual self, we are far from being the source of life to others. This is the nature of creation. Nothing can be gained if we do not understand that the path to happiness, love and success is challenging our ego consciousness. We need to transcend our need for self-gratification and support each other through taking the mantle of unconditional love. If we resist the spirit of unconditional love, it is because we truly do not yet understand our true identity. It is because we do not feel confident and trust from others who are still dead to their spiritual self. It is because we do not feel our love for others will be sufficient to bring the dead alive. It is a numbers game. But equally a quality game. Everyone should play their part.

Why did it take so long for this to reach me? Was I the cause of the delay? Was Nature waiting for me to ask for help? In reality, this could well be the case as Nature only respond to our deepest heartfelt prayers, as I have subsequently discovered. As I read over my notes from this conversation, I finally got it. My life has always been mired with troubles because it was devoid of an understanding of my life's purpose. Love is missing and I must give it freely. I have time to turn around the clock – today is the start of a new day. It can be turned around.

I am grateful that I do not have to die impoverished of love and the key to love has been handed back to me. Knowledge is power if one can implement it correctly. Now it was for me to invoke it. You can do the same in your own life. If you have struggled with the purpose of your life, you now know that love for others unconditionally is the key reason you are here. If you are to be happy, successful and enjoy the gift of love, start loving others unconditionally.

I wondered what life would have been for me if the sages had handed the wisdom to my parents before their divorce. Perhaps it would have helped – I thought silently. Then again, it may have not, as I have seen families in the royal household experiencing marital strife and divorce. This is another trick of the ego's mind working in me. One must be careful of the deadly sin of regret and self-pity. No one is going to escape the journey of life and the challenges to our egos. This is the purpose of life. Everyone has to overcome obstacles to demonstrate their willingness to be part of life itself. Let get clear about this: one could never have answers to these questions no matter the emotional reactions. Nature is law and order, and our feelings cannot change the law.

One must learn to accept what life throws at them. One must learn never to regret the past and stay in the present. The voice of the sages speaks through my mind as I reflect on the conversations. It is hard not to look back or feel a sense of regret – that's for sure. As hard as it is, the sages' wisdom must be mastered. I looked at my family photos and, in tears, asked, what shall I do now? I have made mistakes due to ignorance of Nature's law and its expectations of me. What can one do when they find themselves with this information? This is the million-dollar question you and all readers must ponder. The reality is this: you and I cannot change the past. We can only start acting differently today to invoke a new future. We cannot turn the clock back. Mistakes have been made because we did not know any better. Nature designed it this way. Perhaps it was fate.

All of these emotional roller coasters were my personal internal experience with this session. I needed to do something – at least save my kids and grandchildren from the same hell I had experienced. I knew the only thing I could do was immediately put this information in the form of study materials and books first for myself. I had to share it with my kids as well as close relatives. I needed to, and sure enough, I started making plans to publish this book.

The importance of love is not given sufficient attention in mainstream education. We want peace and happiness, yet their source is relegated to the bottom of our priorities. Humanity needs to know that only love can save us from mass suffering and unhappiness. The purpose of life is to become a source of life. The source of life is love; now I know why all the plants in my home withered during the period of strife. Now I understand why relationships die quickly – the absence of love, which is the source of life, leads to death. Now I understand why poverty exists in war-torn countries and homes – where there is no love, the source of life is cut off. Now I recognise why people are more healthy and happy in an environment where love is practised. Love is the source of life; it has everything that a person needs to sustain their life. Love is magnetic. It draws to us all our supply. With this reflection, I determined that my life's purpose is to give love and create space for others to learn how to love unconditionally. Nature is love, but we are not. The work to be done is to shift one consciousness to be kind and loving to others despite our ego's resistance. Our success depends on kindness to one another.

I hope you have taken on board the core message from this lesson. Your life is given to you to create more life for others. You do so when you give others love unconditionally just as Nature gives you life unconditionally. Your happiness, success and love depend on your capacity to conquer the negative spell of your ego, which will always demand attention for the self as the most important. Until you take on the mantle of unconditional love, the path to good health, good relationships and success will be a very long destination from your current station in life.

Use this time to reflect on what you have read so far and agree some action points to move to the next degree.

Your Personal Reflection Notes

_____

_____

_____

_____

_____

_____

_____

_____

_____

_____

_____

_____

_____

Chapter 2
Is there such a thing called fate, which dictates the cause of my life?

Sages Speak – Nature is a system and network of fundamental laws, which cascade in a special order to reach our world, which is the lowest of the different worlds. Nothing is incidental; instead, laws govern everything. The problem is we do not know the system of laws and we experience life complaining about events ignorant of why they happened. Nothing is accidental, and everything happens for a reason. We do not recognise and understand the system of laws, and this is why in our lives, we behave the way we do – working independently of each other, seeking for self-satisfaction at the expense of others.

Humanity should eventually get to a state where everything is revealed, understood, and everything is known, and there are no incidents in their lives. Fate is the force that obligates. There is fate, and there is no coincidence. It is not a question of whether it will happen or not. If you know the laws that obligate, then the outcomes are known in advance – it is like a computer. If you know computer software, you will know the software outcomes, and there is no exception.

> **"Fate is the force that obligates. As we sow, we reap."**

Another question that will naturally flow from this is whether students of truth designed to attain the source and essence of life can change their fate. A person can study spirituality and still not understand or grasp all the system's laws and forces. As a result, they may not know the events' outcomes or what could happen moment by moment. However, the extent to which they are aware of the laws governing the entire system as well as understand the system that resembles the source of life according to its law, which is revealed – then they will be able to recognise the past, present, and the future as one event.

Sara's Reflection

The subject of fate has never been opened to me in this manner. I never recognised my environment as a system of an integrated network operated by a series of laws independent of my consciousness. I never recognised that this system of laws would deliver results based on my attitude and consciousness, and I cannot influence it to bow to my wishes.

Many of us are expecting to gain without investing in the system of life as Nature expects of us. Many of us, want the laws to change to meet our needs, the very thought itself is problematic. Our cries or complaints about life events will not change the system.

At best, our cries will invoke help to guide us to the path that will lead to an inner transformation and alignment to Nature's system.

Very often, we do not see how Nature is unpeeling the layers of egoism within us, which keeps us separated from the purpose of life. We do not see that the very experiences that we are met with are designed to achieve the ultimate goals of life itself. Nothing makes sense to us when we are far from understanding the laws and how our social and emotional interactions invoke the outcomes we experience. I want to now believe that even our childhood experiences that mould us into an adult are all predestined for a higher purpose. Who knows which camp in the life puzzle a person belongs. All we know is this: life is here and we are part of it. If you reflect on your life, you will begin to see patterns; why are these patterns there? Is it fate? Is it coincidence? Of course the answer is for you to discover. No one can answer these questions for you.

> **"Our consciousness determines our fate; one should aspire to attain a higher consciousness."**

Looking at my childhood experiences that led to many challenges in adulthood, I can see how fate brought me to the point of screaming for help in 2009. No amount of education devoid of spiritual understanding was capable of saving me. I can see very clearly, why strife and conflict permeated my environment as an adult; fate was speaking loud and clear. Fate says: you must change your nature to be like me to escape your predicament; ego says: I am the master of my life and I will do as I please. How many times do we fail to recognise change is needed because we ignore the signals? We do so all the time and err towards blaming others for our inaction as well as failures. There are inner forces within a person that can only manifest the experiences we realise. Until we raise our consciousness and align to unconditional love and kindness to others, we are bound to create collision when these forces are negative in form.

My childhood experiences were predominately my consciousness. Until consciousness changes, there is no hope of bringing order and serenity in a person's life. The same principles apply to everyone. No matter what we believe or think, if we are out of balance with nature's laws, we will suffer the penalties to bring us back in balance. There are some situations where events unfold in a person's life that are unexplainable, possibly due to the absence of all the information to make sense. Overall, one must do their best to bring love and kindness for others in their lives to be in close alignment with Nature.

After this session, I interviewed my two special male friends who were happily married. I asked them questions about how they came to create a happy and successful married life and whether their parents were happily married or not. The two friends merely repeated the same feedback to me, much to my surprise. Neither of them knew each other. Both confessed their parents' marriages were not ideal and perfect for replicating. However, they decided to choose their partners carefully outside the environment they were brought up in. They consciously determined they wanted to care for their spouse's happiness and general well-being. It was essential for them to create a happy home for their children. Against this backdrop, they have always led their homes with the consciousness of love and success in mind. They had challenges with their spouse but always worked through them with their vision for the relationship when it started. Their success in marriage was no accident. As I reflected, fate gives what we are, not what we want to be.

> **"There are no accidents or coincidences. Fate simply obligates."**

Where one operates their lives in opposition to nature's laws, the dire consequences will be experienced with the good intention of cautioning a change in direction. Every action has a consequence. There are no accidents. When decisions are made, we can reasonably predict success and failure if we discern nature's laws. One way to do so is to ask oneself if the decision will lead to doing good to others: if the decision will bring success to others, if the decision will make others happy, if the decision will foster love and kindness to others. If the decisions made by us on a daily basis violate these guidances, we can be guaranteed to meet lots of problems and failures ahead. One cannot sow failure and unhappiness for others and expect to be successful. It is a spiritual law. We are all connected. We gain what we give. Nature operates as an integral system governed by the law of love.

In my own life, making choices in relationships has been less of a conscious decision until my conversation with the sages. Many dysfunctional experiences were due to unconscious decisions that were self-centred and based on greed, distrust, and insecurity. When the drama of wars and conflict is practised as a habit, it can become a reality in one's consciousness. The consequences can be dire, as decisions are made based on unconscious patterns with the inevitable repeated experiences of the old. One pattern I observed up to the age of twenty-six years when I got married is the incredible appetite to make poor choices in relationships but good choices in matters to do with my career. What does fate have to do with this? Of course, it has everything. My life was taking the path to suffering and unhappiness, unbeknown to me at the time. The poor choices in relationships were natural since loving others as I love myself was never practised or felt like a critical success factor. When I began to see the dichotomy that the poor choices of the past were now affecting the path to success, I naturally had to scream for help. Because by this time, I had begun to become aware of the failure consciousness pattern in relationships and seeking avenues for answers to deal with the problem. Fate's obligations can be put in another as fate realises our inner consciousness.

> **"Do not underestimate the power of your environment. Bad environment will not breed good results."**

Our environment matters a lot. It shapes us for good or bad. One cannot sow apple seeds to harvest mangoes. Nature does not work in this manner. We reap what we sow. If we do not like the harvest, we can obligate nature by sowing the right seeds. Nature is not the sower of the seeds. You and I are. That is the way it goes. Nature simply produces our reality based on the qualities of seeds sown. This is the message that I took from this session with the sages and now I should pass this on to you. No matter what we do, if we continue sowing seeds of hate, we will reap the harvest of war and conflict; there is no other option. Laws govern life, and the laws are constant as well as unchanging.

I recount a woman who was having a hard time succeeding in her academic studies. She was constantly met with criticism that she was stupid and lazy. The harsh statements did not help her confidence, and with that, she performed worse than in previous exams. Then one day, someone took her under their supervision. They mentored and coached her. She was so confident; she studied hard, and for the first time, she brought an excellent report of her performance to her parents. She achieved second position in her class that month. She had been at the bottom throughout, and no one expected such a dramatic result. The reason was the environment changed. Fate delivers what the environment sowed in her. Her performance was no accident. Fate being the realisation of the force that obligates was at work in this woman's life. We can never know the totality of a person's consciousness. We simply see manifestations and sometimes we are shocked, surprised and happy depending on what is manifested. Nature is always at work. No one knows what will happen the next hour but Nature is in control. Ours is to play the role we are given in the spirit of love to inject more life in the system we call Nature.

Many factors influence a person's happiness and success. The environment we live and breathe can make or break us. We must put ourselves in an environment that will create success for others and ourselves. Otherwise, we risk experiencing failures and repeated disappointments. To conclude this section, your consciousness matters as it manifests all the time. What you think about others, do for and against others matters. You have nothing to lose and everything to gain upgrading your consciousness for the betterment of others. When you begin to observe the quality of your consciousness closely, you will see the relationships between your life experiences and your inner state.

Use this time to reflect on what you have read so far and agree with some action points to move to the next degree.

Your Personal Reflection Notes

_____

_____

_____

_____

_____

_____

_____

_____

_____

_____

_____

Chapter 3
What stops me from evolving into my greater self?

Sages Speak – What is the greater self? There is no such thing, and it is a sign that a person does not know the purpose of his/her life. Many people pursue different careers and do all sorts of things claiming to seek what will bring them to success. Is this what you mean by your greater self? Are you asking what stops you from becoming the leader or earning the highest remuneration in your professional roles? What do you really mean by your greater self? The question is who told you that the work you do would lead to your greater self? Who told you that you are meant to pursue the profession of your choice? Maybe your whole structure, heart, mind, and feelings are in a different role. You need to know yourself as a person – not look at what others do successfully to determine your career choice. You need to be aware of your feelings – what are you drawn to? A person can only excel in the areas where they are more suited based on how nature designed them.

> **"A person can only excel in the areas where they are more suited based on how nature designed them."**

Some may even ask this question: will studying spirituality, which helps a person attains the quality of Nature, assist a person to determine a successful career path? Spirituality is not a study that deals with our corporeal world. Therefore, it is not likely to help you decide on the career you must pursue for success. This is because it is not designed to assist a person in attaining the optimal career pursuit. Instead, it is a study of how to organise our internal structure to be similar to the upper force (Nature) through the right connection with others.

When one studies spirituality, which for this purpose is defined as the attainment of the source of life – the essence of life itself – their attitude towards life will change for the better. Their attitude towards others becomes more conscious and love centred. However, this does not lead a person towards a particular vocation in their profession. Neither does it guarantee success in a chosen profession. A person will sense if a profession is for them if they remain sensitive to their feelings, minds, and bodies. They will understand the forces of their soul, and with that, they can know if a particular profession is well suited. A person will not go after something that is not in line with the forces of their nature or inner tendency. No satisfaction will be attained, and they will be frustrated and unhappy in their profession.

The most prominent mistake people make in life is to look at others in a career and pursue the same career to achieve relative success. Of course, this is a big mistake because we are different and the person who succeeded in a particular profession is in a place where the forces of their soul support them. If you were to attempt to undertake the same profession, the lack of forces from your soul makes success impossible.

The disappointments and frustrations many face in their lives are due to their internal resources wrong use. People pursue careers requiring internal resources of qualities they do not possess, which brings them to a dead-end and emptiness. Inevitably, resentment, failure, depression, dissatisfaction and frustration set in when they fail to align themselves to the career path that their soul supports. It is worthwhile studying oneself and choosing what aligns with one's nature.

Parents should be particularly aware not to use their children to fulfil their dreams. It is not unusual to find parents controlling the direction of their children's career pursuit in an unhelpful manner and certainly not in line with the child's nature or soul's purpose. For instance, many children who are now adults have found themselves in a career that their parents dictated would be beneficial financially but left them in emptiness and frustration. The quest for financial gain devoid of the inner strength needed to succeed in a particular field is the cause of many frustrated individuals at work. Unless one aligns their internal resources with the career that suits them best, unhappiness will be the result that follows.

The key here is for you to know yourself and follow your bliss. Never seek to become someone else. Always strive to be yourself and look for work you can do easily to offer value to a significant proportion of humanity. Look for opportunities to serve others in love and kindness, using your natural strengths. You will inevitably be a success provided your attitude and competence in the field of endeavour is above average. Attitude is key, and the spirit of delivering your services will make or break an individual.

The vices of being jealous or envious of others should be removed from your mindset to succeed in your work. Of course, constructive envy can help inspire motivation and drive. Many of us have been envious of the greatest in our field of endeavour for the sole purpose of stimulating our personal and professional excellence. Destructive envy is where one wishes to harm others to stop their success – this should be avoided at all costs. Everyone has a place in the universe, and it is your responsibility to find your place. When you do, work at it as though your entire life depends on it. Everyone has a role of significance to play; you simply need to see others as a co-partner for life. Your good relationship with them is key to the unfolding of life's journey.

> *"You and everyone on this planet are important part of nature; all are family of one spirit self."*

The key message here is this: you are a significant part of nature. You are born to unfold the plans of nature. You will never attain your significance if you do not align yourself with the purpose of life, and study yourself enough to know what your soul will support you to do excellently. When you uphold the guidance given here to navigate your life, you will become all that you were meant to be.

Sara's Reflection

Our world operates almost certainly in opposition to nature. Achieving financial success at the expense of service quality is the norm. We seldom think about personal alignment for a job role. We do not check our internal resources match the expectations of a role but yet find it surprising when we do not excel in the role. We accept roles as part of our survival instinct – very few of us are the exception. We struggle to keep up with the demands of work and somehow think our feelings of lack of success is accidental. This conversation with the sages made so much sense to me.

Looking at our global social media today, one cannot help to see the numerous advertisements of moneymaking schemes peddled to the masses who are hungry for wealth and success. One cannot help to see how the culture of seeking the end results in isolation of the vehicle to get there is not only delusionary but fraught with many disappointments. It is akin to a person taking a coach to cruise the world without any means of travelling the oceans. Not only is this person doomed to fail, one would seriously question their sanity. Have you ever asked yourself the question – what internal resources are needed for the roles in your career? We seldom do so. Have you ever found yourself in jobs out of desperation; after a few months, you begin to look for another job because it is not suited? You are not alone. Many do so and never once ask, what are my soul's forces and what job role suits me best?

> **"We live in a world that opposes nature's law. Our role is to conquer the force of opposition and unity in love."**

As I reflect on this further, I cannot help but notice how the ego set us in more darkness not to think about our soul. I cannot help to notice that if one truly focuses on the soul's forces they will also serve others with love, offering excellent products that add value to society. Of course, our greed takes us further from our true nature and keep us from attaining anything but success.

After this lesson, I concluded it is a grave misconception that one can succeed in any career of their choice. It is a fatal error of judgement not to look deep within before making career choices. Our career is not always a reflection of our true nature. Many circumstances can lead us to make choices that are not always in our best interest of ourselves and others. As I was growing up, there were teachers who were excellent at their job and those who had no business in the classroom but were in the profession. This is not only damaging for the poor-performance teachers, their students also suffer since they are ill-suited to bring the best out of them. Praying to achieve excellence in a profession that is unsuited for a person's development, growth and success is also a waste of time. At most, you will attain the wisdom to make a change in career.

> *"Your spiritual attainment is insufficient for career success. You need internal forces to support your job role."*

I recall a friend who struggled in his career as an accountant for many years. When I eventually asked him why he seemed indifferent to his career pursuit, he put it bluntly that his interest had always been in the medical profession, but his parents were not supportive of his choice. His spiritual life is sound and yet he struggled to make a success of his career. This conversation helped me understand what the issues were. I finally made sense of what was going on.

Others finish university and spend years making sense of their true career pursuit. Their dilemmas have nothing to do with their spiritual success or lack of it. One must be willing to pursue a career path that they truly feel drawn to and are satisfied with. When one is confident with their career, they will excel because the spirit with which they deliver their services will be loving and warm. People sense warmth and harmony through services; they also sense the lack of warmth and love when they are not satisfied.

I once had the pleasure of speaking with a friend who had to return to full-time employment after closing his longstanding business. He was deeply hurt by the event and circumstances that led him to give up his self-employment status. He was now in his employment but still angry. Despite all attempts to do his best, he was constantly running into trouble in the last minutes. He could not get his contract confirmed and the frustration continued. He could not immediately figure out the problem; he was hurt yet was engaged in spiritual practices. The wisdom of the sages brought home to me that his problem was twofold. His unwillingness to accept his station in life put him in conflict with nature, which was a no-win situation for him. Nature abhors conflict. The conflict he had internally had to be resolved. Until he resolved it, his energy attracted more conflict, and with that, he could not hold down the roles that he despised.

To succeed in any job role, one must be warm and accepting of the position, even if one is working on something else. No one can be their higher self in a role they despise. In truth, if one practises love across all spheres of their life, one will be able to hold down a job. Let's be clear here – doing good to others is what love means. You cannot do good to others and not experience good. If a person is fired from a job it is because they genuinely do not love the role. When you love something, you want to give your best at it and make others happy.

"Your greater self is the person you can become when you align your spirit to your soul's purpose."

Nature is law and order. When we are not succeeding in a career, it is because we are not aligned to the career. We must align internally with a career to succeed at it. If a career is temporary, we must be aligned with it while working on the alternatives. Otherwise, the lack of warmth and kindness towards the role will be felt by those who receive the service. This same individual eventually was confirmed and given a permanent contract in a third role, but this was not without challenges. When he eventually got the message that his attitude towards his work situation was the cause of his problems, he shifted internally and began giving gratitude to the Creator for the job's blessing. With that, he set into motion his new plans for the role he now wants to pursue in the future. The shift came gradually after he attended another interview for a higher grade role to improve his income. He was declined the role, but the director was strangely willing to meet him for an hour's feedback discussion. This offer to meet with the director who turned him down for the role was rare. He did accept the meeting, and it was an eye-opener for him that day. The director recounted where he was below the expected standard for the role. However, the panel's general view was that he was suitable except for a few areas where another candidate was stronger. Then the big moment arrived; the director recounted that something was undeniable and different about his reactions to different questions. When questions were asked about the technical side of the role (finance matters), he was very agitated, and everyone felt it. However, when questions were asked about leadership, he was very relaxed, and his eyes lit up in ways that they did not experience with the other questions. He was amazed to see the marked difference in the reaction and wanted to ask more questions. The panel felt this, and no doubt was considered in their decision. The friend could not bring himself to tell the director the truth of what underpinned the experience. As they concluded that session, he resolved to move on with the current job and work fervently on his new career plan that he felt drawn to.

All too often, we underestimate the power of our thoughts and think we can disguise them. Unfortunately, our inner world impacts our feelings, which influence our actions. What we do not see is that we cannot escape the way we feel about a situation. We can gloss over them with smiles and nice clothing, but we can never change the energy of our thoughts and feelings. They follow us like clouds, and we are often unaware that we are interacting with other people's energy. At that level, we can never deceive others. It is precisely, for this reason, we can find ourselves failing in one role and succeeding at another – the spirit with which we serve matters.

If we serve in the spirit of hate, anxiety, worry, insecurity, conflict, resentment and anger, our failure is guaranteed. We can never succeed in an environment of disharmony. If we serve with passion and love, our success is guaranteed. A person can be technically sound in an area of work but fail or not excel in the career due to the spirit of their service.

Here is the key message for you and me: our spiritual practices and education will not guarantee success if we do not apply the spirit of love across all spheres of our lives. Offering services we are suited to deliver is part of demonstrating love to others. For this reason, we should be mindful of the risk of pursuing careers for monetary gain exclusively. We need to ensure we plant ourselves in a role where our soul supports us, and we are of service optimally.

I remembered after hearing this how I took stock of many friends and relatives I know who are frustrated in their work lives. They often do not make the connection between what they are doing and what their genuine interest is. These individuals will claim they are spiritual, but they are driven by the money prospect regarding their work choices. Clearly, we can all benefit from this conversation with the sages. The popularity and attractiveness of a role are enticing; we are pleasure seekers. We want fast food, fast sex, fast success, fast money and the list goes on. However, we need to develop the internal capacity to stop the urges and think about others to make meaningful decisions about our service to the world.

I have also experienced failure in my personal life due to extreme and prolonged periods of anguish. One cannot violate nature's laws and succeed. Every experience is a message from nature that we must pay very close attention to our internal state and interactions with others. When one is not succeeding in a specific endeavour, they should quiet their mind's heart to uncover what they feel drawn to. It may not look financially rewarding immediately, but it is better to be involved in work where your soul supports you.

Use this time to reflect on what you have read so far and agree with some action points to move to the next degree.

Your Personal Reflection Notes

_____

_____

_____

_____

_____

_____

_____

_____

_____

Chapter 4
Why is it that I cannot feel truly happy?

Sages Speak – What does it mean to be happy? This is one of the first questions we need to answer. What is happiness? Everyone seemingly wants to be happy. People build for themselves a picture or mould of an actor or celebrity representing an image of happiness. They confuse themselves with the adverts on the television and newspapers of happiness. Thereafter, they discovered the image of happiness they upheld was a sham when the celebrity commits suicide down the line. They externalised happiness as something achieved when one acquires lovely objects such as cars, homes, and so on. Happiness becomes the end, and the objects become the means to attain happiness. This is the flaw of our society today. Happiness and harmony are states of consciousness – they do not depend on the possession of things.

Let's go deeper: things seen as objects are created through the application of the right mental attitude. Things, when created, do not result in a person attaining happiness or harmony. This is so important to know because people think they will be happy when they possess things. This is far from the reality, hence the psychological chaos many suffer. One can apply their mental power and create for themselves all sorts of things only to find they are happy for a few days or months to be followed by prolonged unhappiness. True happiness is a spiritual state – it requires a person to be in wholeness with himself. It requires a person to be in a state of perfection, which is humanity's true nature.

> *"Your happiness has nothing to do with materiality. You are happy when you are connected to the source of life."*

Happiness has nothing to do with the physical objects a person possesses. Happiness is an eternal state – it is precisely why many are not truly happy. This also explains the emptiness found in materially conscious people who naively expect to create happiness by acquiring more money and objects. Of course, you can be financially wealthy and happy if you attain wholeness. Equally, a person can be in a straightforward profession and be happy. Happiness is not the end, but rather the means to an end. As long as a person does not compare themselves with others and be envious of others with the intent to cause harm, they will be in a state of wholeness and perfection with themselves and be happy. One must be connected to others healthily to be happy. Otherwise, unhappiness will be guaranteed.

Malicious envy is the beginning of destruction. Being happy is being in wholeness with one's life. It is not unusual for a person to look back in time and conclude that they were much happier in the past than they are at present. This is the mental activity that puts many in a state of unhappiness. The habit of continually using one's mind to revisit past events, which are glorified as happy relative to the present state will almost certainly keep a person in sadness. As long as the mind is used in this way, a person will create unhappiness in the mind as the ego is at work.

Learning to be present in our mental state helps to avoid the ego's trickster to create unhappiness where it was never needed in the first place. It is also common for the ego to create a future state that will be much happier so that one can never be happy in their present state. This habit of the mind keeps many in a state of unhappiness since they continue to work for a future state. Being present helps to conquer the ego's mind game of creating future dreams that are never realised, keeping us on a mental treadmill.

> *"Stay present. Avoid the trap of a mental treadmill holding you to a future desired state. The NOW is all you will always have."*

Our ego is the source of our unhappiness. It is an opposing force that seeks for the self and not for others. It is always judging negatively and making more demands for more self-pleasure and showing us many lacks. Left unchecked, it wants to devour the world. This ego is in all of us, and we must get to know how it works in us. If you do not understand the ego in you and how to work with it, life will be hell on earth as you will never be in wholeness and perfection with yourself.

As our ego grows, without a person balancing their lives with the force of unconditional love for others, their capacity to resemble the upper world's quality (spiritual world) diminishes. Simply put, a person becomes more selfish and self-centred with time. Without a constraint over this evil nature, to counteract it with love for others, unhappiness is a guaranteed outcome. A person can never be happy if he/she does not make others happy. Selfishness is an act of seeking your happiness at the expense of others.

Even so-called wealthy celebrities do not understand that this is what is happening to them. Many have lots of money but no happiness because they are so self-consumed. Many people in our world do not know this is what is happening to them. They are not taught in schools to be wary of the vices of seeking for themselves at the expense of others. People become a victim of the commercialism of all sorts due to their ignorance of the source of happiness. Those who crave the best designer bags, shoes, cars, vacations and the list goes on, expecting to find happiness there, only find emptiness after going through the charade. None of these things will ever give them happiness because the state of happiness is imprinted on one's soul. When people connect at the soul level, they will attain happiness. Happiness is the product of the connection between people at their soul level.

> **"The state of happiness is imprinted on one's soul. No one can attain happiness through material objects. It is a product of the healthy connection between people."**

Unhappiness is a negative emotion that signals a change is needed; the signal is often misinterpreted. A person who discerns their life – why they were created, and why people live and die as a life cycle – becomes much calmer. He understands that the purpose of life is to attain the source of life (love), and with that, does not sign up for all sorts of philosophy that confuse the mind and create unhappiness.

People who take examples from others' lives will ultimately live in others' desires. They will live in the goals that others have created for them. This, of course, implies the wishes of others are not yours. As a result, such people will always be unhappy. They do not operate in their own forces and they are not in wholeness and perfection with themselves.

Envy and jealousy of others are indicators that one is dissatisfied with their lot. Such individuals are ignorant of the purpose of their lives, and are unable to live in the present state. This will result in one constantly living in the future. Such people are drawn by their futuristic images created by the desire to become someone else other than themselves. The result of all the above is unhappiness.

The solution is to learn how to discern oneself, one's soul life force, how to harness it and live life in line with nature's law. No experience of unhappiness will arise when this solution is put in place.

Many laws are operating in the universe, and the law of growth is one of them. The egoistic desires of humankind will always grow. This is good as it creates the potential for advancement. Be cautious not to be carried away with desires that are likely to align you with professions ill-suited to maximise your soul forces.

For this reason, seek first to be whole and perfect through the right connection with others. Seek first to be in alignment with nature's laws, and with this, the rest of your life will unfold naturally. This is because you will become more sensitive to your natural forces and inclination. You will be able to find the right profession, partner and friends to maximise your soul's forces.

Sara's Reflection

I wish this subject was taught in schools and universities where the opportunity to practise and develop life skills was ripe. It does not take a genius to figure out very quickly why there is so much unhappiness in our world if we are all so busy looking for the next thing or the next person that will make us happy.

After reflecting on this session, I can now understand why most people spend more time feeling sorry for themselves when faced with life's challenges such as a loss of a loved one, marital breakup, business failure and more. These challenges are often devoid of a deeper understanding and with that, we feel saddened by them. Of course, happiness should be a target in all relationships, but it is taken for granted. Most people think it will happen without mutual investment in relationships. This is the flaw in our human relationships, which very often comes back to haunt us.

> **"Love is like an animal. If you do not feed it with the right food it will die. Relationships need love to survive."**

We assume that the other's role is to make us happy. We think they should sacrifice their desires and hopes for ours while we do nothing. Of course, nature will not have it that way as we are all expected to be whole and perfect.

My deep reflection caught sight of one of my relatives who has a habit of sharing personal matters in the public domain. The family member once ventured to do so with a friend of mine. I had no idea this had happened until I received a call from my friend. My friend shared some of the personal details divulged, much to my surprise. I was embarrassed, stunned, and speechless. My friend informed me that this relative is depressed. She was implying I was the cause of her emotional traumas. I quickly responded that I do not wish to discuss these matters as they were family issues and should be private and confidential. I wondered why my relative somewhat felt I was responsible for their unhappiness. After some reflection time, I took the matter to God and asked for her healing. Perhaps the only gift of happiness I can give my relative is God's hands on the matter that troubled her. After I did so, I left the matter, and over time, everything went back to normal. I could not change the events of the past and erase their impact on her. However, I can do something today to ensure her needs for happiness are met. Prayer was what I used on this occasion.

Through prayers, I have seen many of the issues that I felt unhappy about change. By sending prayers for others I automatically shift my thoughts to the needs of others and become one with their desires. I share this because, sometimes we delude ourselves that others are responsible for our happiness. In reality, we are responsible to help others be happy. When we do so, happiness will be our state of mind.

> *"We attain happiness when we make it our mission to make others happy. Just do it."*

The ego-mind will often justify why we should be more concerned about our opinions over others. We should not justify the demands for us to support others and keep us in conflict. I have cited many occasions where this could have been my position had I not been in this conversation with the sages. Love is the ultimate goal of our life. Without the act of love shown to others, we can never connect with them and create happiness.

We have to remind ourselves of the spiritual goals constantly that we wish to live by. Otherwise, we will endanger the importance of connecting healthily with others and create unhappiness. No matter what one gains physically, if it is obtained at the expense of others' happiness, then our own unhappiness will await us as life unfolds.

Use this time to reflect on what you have read so far and agree with some action points to move to the next degree.

Your Personal Reflection Notes

Chapter 5
What can be done to improve my relationships with others?

Sages Speak – Many people are disturbed by the nature of their relationships, whether it be family, spouse, colleagues, boss, neighbours, and friends – they want to improve them but feel lost. Fundamentally, we have forgotten the importance of forgiveness. Humanity has been given this formula to improve relationships for millennia, and yet ignores it and continues complaining and fighting with each other.

Let us start by defining forgiveness for this session to ensure you are clear about its importance. Forgiveness is the act of covering an offence with love for unity and harmony. Forgiveness acknowledges a transgression but chooses to let go of it to build a good connection with others. Through forgiveness, we master love and heal rifts between people. We must return to the first principle – the art of forgiveness. Forgive others relentlessly. Forgive yourself, relentlessly. Just as you want to be forgiven, you must learn to forgive in relationships. If we know how to do this properly, we will live a happy life.

We are all small people thrown from one state to another. We need to remember that we are egoists at the core of our nature, and many are still unconscious of their higher selves. We need to lower our expectations of others and forgive. People swing from one state to another, which are indicators of nature working in a person. Spirituality teaches us to love thy neighbour as thyself because that which we see as people outside us is truly within us. It is this inner world we are to correct to create the perfect world of happiness we seek. This is fundamentally why forgiveness must be practised doggedly if one wants to improve their relationships with others.

> *"We are all small people who are operating below our state of perfection. Forgiveness must be practised daily."*

There is no other way – forgive, forgive, and forgive! When you forgive, correction takes place within, and the world outside you will change. Why? What lies outside is perfect. What lies within you is the source of imperfection that should be corrected. The ego within seeks for the self and wants to disconnect from others. This is a force that creates conflict between people.

Some people have severe problems with forgiveness; they see it as a weakness that others will abuse. They see it as a weakness because they will be expected to forgive when others continue their abusive conduct. Of course, forgiveness does not mean that one should expose themselves to future abuses and certainly, it is not an act of weakness.

The capacity to act higher than one's environmental condition is a strength as the natural thing to do is act in line with one's environmental conditions. There is a deeper knowing that comes when one begins to embrace forgiveness – it is hard to explain the process. You have to feel it yourself. Remember, the ego's self-love program drives our internal environmental conditioning, and until the program is upgraded, nothing will change on the outside.

Forgiveness is the key to make a correction. It is the means of connecting with others wholly, in the spirit of love. It is the means of behaving like the source of life – Nature. It is the means of breathing life into the environment through love. Forgive and move on – do not give occasion for the negative behaviour to continue by being a party to the event.

Of course, this is not always possible, particularly in a family situation – by this, I mean, you cannot abandon your family physically. However, you can love them and create a space for them to be themselves, practising non-judgement. Relationship is the means through which you attain the quality of the source of life. Forgiveness is the tool you use to get there. In a life-threatening situation such as violence, sexual abuse of all types, do your very best to forgive and keep a long physical distance that will protect you from the destructive behaviour of others. However, love is always to be practised and mastered.

Many of the ailments our society suffers are rooted in unforgiveness. Lack of forgiveness has been shown to cause emotional negativity such as anger and resentment, which then become the cause of stress and diseases. We cannot afford not to forgive others. We cannot become happy when we hold unforgiveness in our hearts. We cannot achieve the greatest self or our life purpose with unforgiveness as a lifestyle – nature does not allow it. We have to love one another, and that means to forgive one another. Practical steps to reduce the abuse can be taken, but forgiveness must be mastered.

All our spiritual books for generations have shown that no spiritual attainment or connection with the higher force was ever possible while in unforgiveness. The instruction to love thy neighbour as thyself is rooted in this demand for forgiveness. If we do not forgive, our Father in heaven will not forgive us. Forgiveness brings us closer to the Creator, as it is an act of love for the offender.

> *"Our relationships with others will always test our love for others as ourselves. Forgive to heal. Forgive to connect."*

Forgiveness changes the quality of a person to become similar to Nature. It is an act of love towards another. We often confuse love as something to receive and not to give. Love and hate are in the same spectrum. There can never be love without hate. Hence, our sages said – love covers all transgression. If we do not forgive, we will also find that we are in the same mental and spiritual imprisonment that we confined those we hold in unforgiveness.

Forgiveness is not a luxury if you are serious about attaining the purpose of your life. As hard as it might be, it is a necessary tool to demonstrate 'Love thy neighbour as thyself'.

Sara's Response

Our biggest challenge will always be revealed through the relationships between us. There is nothing we can ever achieve independent of relationships. We are so tied up together through Nature, we rarely understand we are far from being independent. To be independent is to die a natural death as such a phenomenon does not exist. Nature is integral and so are we. All our aspirations for happiness, success, good health and love are intricately knitted through the web of our interrelationships. This means, a person cannot ignore the importance of good relations. You and I do so at our peril. Nature has created a masterpiece hidden from the eyes of humans.

After my conversation with the sages, I took a good look around me and discovered that every part of the system called Nature is connected to another seamlessly. Fundamentally the system caters for our sustenance through the relationships between the different parts of the system. The system is rich and full but its richness is unattainable. If one does not hold the quality of fullness and richness within, they will be prone to act in opposition to the system. This will then stop the flow of supply to the different parts of the system. To be full within, a person must be aligned wholly to Nature's law of love. A person should be in a state of love for others and have no concern for the self. Remember, everyone should be in this state of love for Nature's gift of love to be realised. But there is a problem; we are not acting in fullness. The ego shifts us inward, paints a picture of independence and individualism. With this picture, we like weaklings fall under its spell thinking and acting for the self, damaging the relationships between us and stopping the flow of our supply and sustenance.

> **"A person must conquer their egos to build healthy relationships with others."**

All living beings have lower-order needs. Humans for instance need food, sex, money, family, honour and wealth. As a result, we can never achieve these goals without personal mastery in our relationships with each other. If we fail to maintain good relationships with the different parts of the system, failure is inevitable. Failure comes in the form of poor relationships with family members, workmates, employers, different countries, tribes within countries, spouse, neighbours as well as with the animal kingdom, the plant kingdom and the earth. Everything that the system needs for our existence is available but can only be accessed through the right relationships between all parts of the system.

With this realisation, I began to take a good look at my life. I looked at the lives of others and wondered why we are all not masters of good relationship. We are challenged by our egos desire to devour everything and leave nothing for others. The importance of spiritual education became profound in my consciousness. I got it; there is only one way to access the state of happiness, love and success. One should transform their inner egoistic state into an altruistic state. This should be done through a heart connection, which cares for everyone in the system called Nature and not just for oneself. We are to seek for others' best interests and not just ourselves. But how can we do this? Education in relationship that opens the heart connection with others. A person can have a cordial and warm relationship with the intent to use others for their selfish benefits. This is of course not going to help the system. Nice words and smiles that are through the intellect will take no one very far. True relationships begin with a melting heart. The act of forgiveness is truly one that demands a melting of the heart to reach love.

This session was one of the best for me as it brought home the importance of kindness to others. I finally got it; it is impossible to develop good relationships with others if we do not conquer our ego and its harsh judgements. It is impossible to open one's heart to others if one is unwilling to accept human nature's vulnerability.

The majority of our experienced conflicts stem from the lack of understanding of where we fall in the spectrum of the perfection of nature. It also demonstrates a lack of awareness of life's journey to the highest point in the ladder of consciousness. Our life could be much happier if we only understand that the purpose of life itself is to support one another to become the best versions of ourselves. That ideal version is not achieved overnight, and with that, our expectations should be much lower than we often set them when dealing with people. This means one should be cautious in relationships to maintain the right balance to ensure all parties' safety.

I now realised the importance of studying the nature of people in my life and ensuring the right boundaries are set while at the same time being loving and kind. This has helped me tremendously as previous frustrations were born out of my ignorance of the human race's fragility and Nature's system. In hindsight, I should have known that my tendencies can be a mixture of great and not so great; others have the same and should not be expected to demonstrate a saint's status all the time – if at all. We could all save ourselves the pain of arguments over minutia with this understanding in mind.

Belabouring the vices of others is the most unproductive action one could engage in. It is a sure way to stop the flow of energy in the system of Nature. Every part of the system should connect. Our relationships are stronger with mutual understanding, care and support for one another.

The sudden realisation that the frustrations we very often experience in many of our relationships are born out of ignorance hit me in the face. We think we are independent of each other, whereas Nature has designed us to be dependent on each other for our general well-being and success. We think we can disconnect from each other without significantly hurting ourselves. Yet nature dictates the opposite. Our disconnect stops the flow of supply through the system and keeps us in lack of supply. Wherever you find excess egos in action, you will find conflicts and poverty manifesting in different areas of the system. Generally, this shows up as wars, financial troubles, disputes, marital breakdown, ill health in the different ecosystem, poor harvests and more. Love is the ultimate goal to strive for to maintain good relationships. Healthy relationships connect us to the perfection of Nature. Bad ones do the reverse. If you and I are truly seeking love, happiness and success, the ultimate goal we should strive for is good connection between us. This means, we must become masters of forgiveness to spread love like a wildfire.

> **"Our relationships with others will always be tested. Love glues good relations. Forgive to heal. Forgive to connect."**

Good relationships are tasking to us as they require our investment of time and effort to conquer our egos. They require us to demonstrate self-discipline. Listening attentively to others and fulfilling the desires of others are a tall order for our egos. For you to attain higher consciousness, try embracing small acts of kindness to others until habit becomes nature.

Use this time to reflect on what you have read so far and agree with some action points to move to the next degree.

Your Personal Reflection Notes

_____

_____

_____

_____

Chapter 6
Why do bad things happen to good people and vice versa?

Sages Speak – It all depends on the fate of a person. There is nothing we can do about it. If we see someone earning millions on the stock exchange and we are losing on the same day, we must acknowledge we do not know the laws that govern the system. We do not know the network of all the laws, and if we were to know the network of laws, we would make no errors. One who does not err is a beast. Animals do not make errors. If something happens to an animal, according to the law of nature, that is how it is meant to be. Animals make decisions based on their instinct and are usually correct.

As humans, we make errors because we are clueless about the network of laws and forces that govern nature's system and controls them. We have to figure out how to work correctly in our environment for the betterment of self and others. We have to discover the laws of nature and invoke them to raise consciousness. We are different from other creations. We co-create with Nature and to this extent, we are unique. We are in a network of many forces. However, we do not know them. The beams of these forces are innumerable and working on every cell and system within us – emotionally, physically, and mentally. We do not know them, which is why we make mistakes.

The wisdom of nature that shows us how to receive and understand this whole system that manages us slowly enables us as a child, youth, adult, and man, and reveals how these forces work. A person who has attained spiritual enlightenment will usually see some of these forces depending on their attainment. When the wisdom of nature is revealed, these networks of forces will begin to change our life for good.

> *"What is good? To be a good person is to live above one's default egoistic nature. To be a bad person is to live in the ego consciousness."*

You may ask what it means to be good. What does good mean? To be good is to be above our default egoistic nature, which is considered bad. A person, as an egoistic creature, thinks only about themselves. They think of how to use others and destroy them. They do not think about how to help others succeed but rather how to devour everything for oneself. Divide and conquer are the principles for living until one is awakened and transforms spiritually in the quality of unconditional love – like Nature. Therefore, a person is managed by the forces of the upper world.

This is because the upper is the purest existence. The upper world represents wholeness and love for all creations.

All the bad that exists is the product of the self-love quality that we possess. Self-love keeps us in darkness and it is the opposite quality of Nature – unconditional love. If we were to remain in our egoistic state, which is growing steadily without being tamed, we would head for a serious crisis. This is the reason for many of the bad things we experience in our world. They are there to awaken us to change our nature. They are there to awaken us to observe Nature as an integral system of love. They are there to instigate an inner revolution towards perfection. They are there to bring us closer to a healthy state of heart connection.

We have to correct our nature. As humans, we are not created solely to acquire a fortune and remain like beasts looking for the next conquest. Rather humanity was created to seek everything that will bring them to love for others. Love for others brings us into the perfect state of happiness, success and joy. When humanity attains this love, the heart's eyes will be opened, and we will see a different spirit within. The heart's mind and ears will be awakened and we will feel the connection between us. The opening of the heart ultimately brings us closer. Whilst in the ego, the heart is closed and we are under the governance of Nature.

> **"We are managed by Nature because our qualities are in opposition to Nature. The bad we see is a reflection of our ego qualities."**

We are all from a system called the soul. It is a round system in which we are all in, and we are all connected by an endless string of forces, which run across every one of us like cells in the body. We are in an integral system – like a small cell within the soul.

We need to learn the system. If we learn how we are connected and benefit our state in the right connection, we will live a good life. We will be in eternal perfection, completion, and wholeness, which is the state we describe in our world as happiness. If we do not connect correctly in the system, we are subjected to pressures for correction. This is what we call a bad state and left unchecked creates suffering.

Sara's Response

The profundity of this lesson was overwhelming. I was taken into a new world in which everything was perfect. The entire system of Nature resurrected in my consciousness; suddenly I observed the synchronicity of creation. It was an eye-opener. The entire system of Nature in which everything exists is harmonious. Everything works perfectly. The only virus to the system is humans. I use the word virus because humans behave opposite to the perfect system. Humans have ego consciousness, which creates a split mentality of duality and opposition. With this imperfection, humans are relegated below the state of perfection. Until we rise in consciousness, we are below the blanket of the perfect state the sages refer to as Nature's integral system.

The entire recognition that the turbulence we experience is nothing more than our ego's disruptive forces in the system was mind-blowing. Nature is a force that is unchanging; it is seamlessly good. We as humans are not in alignment with the totality of Nature's goodness. As a result, we experience the forces of Nature as a pressure on our internalities. It is similar to a person who is told to be kind and nice to others but elects to harm them. This is a disruption to the system particularly when billions of humans are doing the same.

On reflection, I realised, the lack of consciousness of the system that governs us is our biggest obstacle. It has been clouded by many false beliefs and cultural norms over the years. As people we condemn each other and denigrate the value of love, justice and respect for all. We believe in the superiority of certain races and justify demeaning those we believe are of an inferior race. We justify demeaning genders we perceive as weak and the consequences of our actions are rarely seen through our ego lens. Ignorance of the law is no excuse. Nature's door of abundance at all level will only be opened with the correct master key.

> **"You are in two worlds but yet you recognise one without the other. Nature is perfect. Egoism is a system that corrupts the state of the human experiences."**

Our ignorance of Nature is akin to a person who lacks the grasp of the power of electricity. Electricity is a powerful resource. It can light up an entire country, harness numerous technological development, improve the social and economic well-being of societies, as well as many more benefits. Equally, it can be used to destroy and kill when channelled through a system designed to harm others – for instance the electric chair. Whether or not humanity benefits from electricity depends on the channel or system through which it passes. Electricity gives humanity the results of a system's function. We are microsystems in nature's integral macro system. We have the entire world inside us in consciousness and experience it through our multifaceted interactions, which is complex and mired by egoisms. We will generate good outcomes or bad ones based on our consciousness.

Nature is a good force just as electricity is. Nature is present all around us just as electricity. We do not see electricity but we experience its essence. Until one understands the goodness of electricity, as well as its vices when used incorrectly, there is always the risk of abuse with serious consequences. Similarly, there is also the risk that those who are not prepared to construct a beneficial system to access electricity will continually remain cut off from its supply. Nothing is an accident or coincidence.

For humanity, the system to access the perfect state of Nature is the technology the sages have given us – '**Love Thy Neighbour As Thyself'.** We may not always know how to love, but we should endeavour to understand what it means to exit the ego and love others unconditionally. Love is the medicine to heal the virus of egoism that corrupts the beautiful paradise of Nature. We all suffer from this disease. It manifests in the form of chaos and confusion in our lives – ill health, financial troubles, floods, diminished harvests, wars, conflicts, insecurities and more. Deep down in our soul consciousness, we know happiness and harmony are our true state. Our spiritual root is being blinded by egoism leading us to chase materialism to find the perfection of our true state. We do so at the expense of building a community of healthy relationships with people in our homes, workplaces, towns, cities, countries and the world as a whole. Sooner or later we discover the quest is hopeless since no material object is capable of satisfying the spiritual self that is disconnected from the source of life. We can never be truly successful, happy and in joy relying on material toys designed to reinforce individualism. We can never escape the hurdle of building good relationships to sustain our happiness.

All of us are part of the gigantic ego consciousness system; we share the suffering created whilst a significant proportion of the human race is sleeping to their true self. My hope is that this book will help you and many others begin the awakening process. We cannot afford the expensive dream that tricks us into believing love, happiness and joy will manifest through our egoistic connection. Bricks and mortar and all the fancy objects we entertain are only needed for our physical existence. They can never satisfy the soul. They can never replace the part of us that needs each other to soar into the perfect state of Nature. This is a dream that will never come true. This is akin to believing the electric chair will transform human behaviour for the betterment of the whole. The chair was not designed to deliver this outcome and it would be a foolish approach to entertain. Our egoism is a programme within that delivers evil outcomes. When we transform spiritually, the good programme will overlay it and transition us into a good and better world – the world that Nature wishes for us to attain. We cannot fool Nature. Until we create the internal device to access the perfection of Nature, we will remain in darkness. A tree is known by its fruits, which is why we can never fool Nature.

> *"We cannot fool Nature. A tree is known by its fruits. When we take the form of Nature's quality we will manifest the perfect state of Nature."*

I remembered how a flash of the two worlds felt in me when this came to my awareness. It is as though one system is in a state of harmony and the other in a state of conflict. The state of harmony is critical for our salvation. When we say bad things happen to us, we never fully understand how the system of Nature is managing us to bring perfection and wholeness. We focus on the manifestation, ignoring the source and its purpose. With this, one has to really question the judgement of good and bad. If the bad appears, what should we do to overcome quickly? This was my thought. I wonder what you think given what you have read so far.

As humans, our experiences seen through the ego's lens are interpreted as bad if we do not gain pleasures and vice versa. As long as we perceive through the ego sensor, our life experiences fluctuate between good and bad. On the other hand, nature knows only goodness and operates with us through the consciousness of love. If we could only bring ourselves to perceiving through the same consciousness as nature, there will be no duality in our world. Our work of raising consciousness begins from this point. Nature has given us the opposite experiences to instigate another program in the system that will elevate us to see the opposite and understand creation better.

> **"We are all from a system called the soul. It is a round system. We are all connected and what we do affects the entire system for good or bad."**

Let me share a story with you. I once heard something that left me wondering how little we know or understand about our world. A woman adopted a child who she loves dearly, but the child never knew he was adopted until his early teens. When the child discovered he was not a natural child of that woman, he began asking questions about his birth mother. The woman had no idea where the birth mother lived as they had no contact after the adoption for obvious reasons. After much nagging about the son's desire to meet his birth mother, the woman promised that he would certainly be introduced to her when he turned eighteen years old. The matter was settled, and everything returned to the norm. On the day the son turned eighteen, he was involved in an accident and died. The woman was very distraught and bitter after the event of her son's death. After many months of suffering, she made enquiries about the son's birth mother. To her surprise, she got to know that his birth mother had died a few years back. At the time she promised, she had no idea this had already happened, and it would not be possible for her son to connect with his birth mother physically when he turned eighteen. In the period she was emotionally distraught, she lamented that there was no fairness in the system and she would never connect with God due to her experience. Of course, she has limited knowledge of nature's work. After discovering that her promise to the son did materialise, her perception of the event changed completely.

> **"The bad we see is there to awaken us to create the good we want to experience. Our perception of good and bad is questionable"**

Many times, we do not understand the complexity of nature's work. Our self-gratification mindset gets in the way of our judgement, and we think very little of other possibilities that could be at work in the grand scheme of events. Do we really know what is good or bad? Do we know the big picture and how all things work together for good in the system we call planet earth? Our perception of reality is undoubtedly limited.

I remember another event where all my plans were scuppered, leaving me empty and bewildered. I had accepted the inevitable end to my predicament and thought the event would end in less than two years from the date of the occurrence. Nothing prepared me for the protracted conflict with numerous court hearings to untangle complex financial matters involving many parties and missing facts that I was oblivious to. My dreams of restarting my life sooner were consigned to the abyss of nothingness, and with that, I was left wondering if this was fate and what happens next. Was the Creator of the universe trying to tell me something and if so, what was the message? Four years after this event, I was nowhere closer to untangling these financial matters. I became an investigator and an angry person who could not understand her fate. Why did it have to be this way and what should I do to limit the damaging impacts of these matters? Another two years passed and by this time, we were in the sixth year of a protracted investigation and arguments. Finally, I made up my mind to give the smallest attention to the matter and continue with my life. What happened next startled me. I uncovered so many problems that were not known to me during the numerous financial activities. I remember looking back in awe, wondering how the entire event could have gone past my awareness.

One by one, I began to unpick the matters that were the cause of disputes. As we progressed, I began to learn more about myself. Some would have said the event was bad for me and was a great misfortune given the unpleasantry and financial damages. I will say differently; the unfolding events were the greatest gift from the heavens to bring home some important learning points about setting boundaries in relationships. These events were all instrumentally the impetus for a life-transforming change. I had to find solutions outside my immediate environment. I had to learn from a trusted, reputable environment. I learnt very quickly that my childhood's conflict was playing up all over again, despite my determination in the quest for happiness.

Was it fate that I struggled with relationships until I came to this point of conversing with the sages? Were all the unpleasant events to me bad when, in reality, they brought me to a point where the truth was revealed about life, its purpose, and my responsibility as co-partner? I have reached a point where I concluded the events were intended for my greater good. Despite the unpleasantness of the journey, which created many bumps and detours in my living conditions, viewed through the ego's lens, many would say they were bad events. However, I concluded there was never a bad event when viewed through the lens of Nature. In fact, the events were intended for good. I did uncover personality weaknesses. It moved me and all those involved to a higher consciousness required to attain life's purpose. Some are still struggling to get there. But the ultimate goal was to bring order were disorder existed.

> **"Every experience you and I go through is a transformation of our egoism towards the purpose of life. To this end, all is good."**

Often, we judge based on our limited perception and remain clueless of the inner transformational shift an event created in a person's life for the better. We see through our inner mental construct, which sees the world upside down or worse, and the sooner we acknowledge this, the better. Nature is the governing powerhouse. We are operated upon, and we are at best stewards of the physical possessions we delude ourselves will bring us sustainable happiness. Our fixation on gains and losses using physical possessions as the metric poses a real challenge. We should use our relationships as the true metric for success. Our human relational experiences are the journey we must walk to attain the purpose of life. As unpleasant as they may be or not, we must overcome all of them. This is why we need supports. This is why we must be in an environment where we support each other in love.

I once heard a woman's story who had two kids that she lost with her parents on the early morning of Christmas. She was in such great pain and anguish after the event and was monitored closely for suicidal tendencies. Life made no sense to her after that event as her pain grew stronger. I am sure many will ask, why her? She is a nice woman with two beautiful children, so why her? During her interview about the event, she said something very profound. She wished she had not kicked up a fuss about the types of food her children ate. She was very health conscious. She wished all of her fuss was not there at the time; life is bigger than the things she treated as her priority. She confessed, the event created such a big void inside her. She eventually began searching for the meaning of life. She began turning for more answers, inward, and externally. This same event many labelled as bad brought her to the point where she became spiritually conscious.

"Do we really know what is good or bad? Something for you to ponder. We are spirit beings mastering the human experience."

Every event in our world is given to heighten our spiritual consciousness. These events will be experienced through the ego in the first instance at the very least. We may feel suffering, but in reality, no one is falling off the cliffs. Everyone is rising upwards in consciousness as nature operates through us with intent to bring us to goodness.

To conclude, it may seem like our determination of what is good or bad is almost certainly a limiting perception with a physical focus. When we shift to an internal higher consciousness, we experience the fuller and richer goodness of nature very quickly.

Nature's ways are not ours. Nature is good, and we must define good as unconditional love towards others. We do not see the internal constructs of a person nor do we know what corrections are needed to bring one closer to perfection. To end, we must never forget that Nature is a good force. We manifest our experiences based on the egoistic structures within that needs correction. Our life mission is to attain spiritual transformation that will lead us to wholeness as well as happiness, harmony and love.

Use this time to reflect on what you have read so far and agree with some action points to move to the next degree.

Your Personal Reflection Notes

_____

_____

_____

_____

_____

_____

_____

_____

Chapter 7
What is love?

Sages Speak – The upper world that we call nature or God is operated by the principle of love – everything stands on love. The trouble is we do not know what love is. We are doomed by the media that continues to propagate all sorts of images of pseudo-love. If we know what love is, all the expectations that confuse us will be thrashed in one go. Our life will be much calmer. We will tame our expectations of others, recognising our struggles for perfection.

Most people think romantic love is unconditional love. No, this is not unconditional love. At best, you can say it is an emotional chemical at work, in which two people trade off their needs for pleasure – you give me this, and I give you that. However, when the rules of the trade change, each is prepared to leave the relationship or manipulate the other for personal advantage. For instance, if one complains that their partner does not give the gift of flowers anymore or cook the nice dishes enjoyed when they started dating, conflict emerges. Left unresolved, separation is inevitable. Generally, if people cannot overcome their differences, this is a sign, it was not true love in the first place.

> **"True love covers all transgression. When people cannot overcome their differences it is a sign it is not true love."**

Love is not what we think. Love is considered when all the single cells in the body work integrally to support the others. If the right connection ceases between bodily cells, we call this condition toxic. Can you now think or see what love is when it happens between people? Can you see that love is not about what you receive, but rather what you give? Can you see that if everyone operates in love, the world you inhabit would be like paradise? Can you see the problems we have in our relationships that we call love? Many relationships fall way below the mark of true love.

Put another way, when we do not love, we infect ourselves and our world with the same condition. It manifests in our personal reality in the form of conflicts, diseases, wars, divorce, separation, ill-temper, anxiety, depression, resentment, guilt, anger, shame, frustration, despair, loneliness, envy, insecurity, sadness, and the list goes on.

Many of the problems we have are due to the lack of love in our lives. If we can learn this subject well and master its implementation, we will eradicate the millions of dollars going towards social security, mental health facilities, and prisons. Our societal problems are due to the lack of love for one another because we see each person as an independent entity that we have no connection with except for our transactional relation.

People think that self-love is lacking, but this is not true. We love ourselves more than we love others. Whatever we do, we tend to do it for ourselves first, before we think about others. Even when we stay silent over a matter that concerns others, we do so in our own interest though we may disguise the reasons in all shades. Therefore, we are not lacking self-love but rather love for others.

Think about it this way: we are like cells in the one gigantic body we call spirit or nature. We have a designated function to play in this arena, such as to ensure we operate harmoniously, giving to others that which we are capable of in the spirit of love. If we live our lives in a way that supports others, and everyone operates in this way, there will be no need to seek for self at the expense of others. We will be acting for the mutual benefit of the whole. In other words, there will be a special agreement between us, something akin to a mutual guarantee to serve the other for the benefit of all humanity. The special agreement to serve the interest of others when invoked is the force we call love.

> **"Love is considered when all the single cells in the body work integrally to support the others."**

A healthy body is synonymous with cells that operate in this manner, and the reverse is what we experience in an unhealthy body. When we do not invoke the spirit of love, we create disharmonious conditions in the cells within, and that means no positive force of love flows between the cells. The cells shrivel and begin to die slowly due to a lack of nourishment. We feel it in the form of pain and other disease conditions given elaborate names in our medical society. The best medicine humanity can give itself every day is love. Medication will help ease pain in physical bodies, but it will never heal the spirit that is not operating in love.

Watch nature, it speaks to us silently, but we do not listen to the message. We take medication to heal an organ and then we have side effects and complain about the drug's efficacy. This is nature telling us that the best we can do with the physical drug is to suppress or induce a nervous secretion to stop feeling the pain of self-love. Until we get it right, the current status quo will be unchanged.

Love is the right connection between all parts of nature. Love means I understand how you are to be operated and I joyfully seek to fulfil your desires. For our society to flourish, the act of love should be reciprocal, which will lead to wholeness that permeates our world. Therefore, love goes beyond the physical. It is a heart connection. It is a union with the spirit within and Nature's mind. Can you now understand what love is? Do you think about others; the needs of others in your daily life? When you go to shops to buy goods and are searching for deals, do you think about how they were produced? Do you think about the exploitation of farmers and child labour in developing countries? Do you think about the pollution in their environment that causes early death and other societal issues? Do you think about the consequences of the actions to the entire universe – ecosystem worldwide? Well, if you do, you have love in you.

Our life is such that we rarely think of others; nature wants us to love others as we love ourselves. This means, do unto others as you would like it done unto you.

> **"Love is the right connection between all parts of nature. Love means I understand you and I want to satisfy your needs."**

We see lots of breakdowns in relationships because we are not adequately educated on the subject of love. We learn about love from our immediate environment, and unfortunately, most of what we learn is nothing close to the truth of love. The sad truth is, we repeat the ill education we learn from childhood throughout our lives. Nature does its best to push us towards the truth – usually, through various events that we perceive as bad luck or misfortune because we are not ready to love.

Nature operates with two forces: positive and negative. The positive is the giving force, and the negative is the receiving force. To invoke the force of love, there has to be the opposite. There has to be a lack of love to demonstrate love in a relationship. This is how nature is built and the sooner you and the rest of the world know this, the better. Are you shocked by this statement? I would not be surprised if you are. Love and hate are the same in a single continuum. Most people have a lopsided view of how a relationship should be because of our egoistic nature for self-seeking pleasures.

Let us look at an illustration of love in practice. Let us imagine that you concluded that someone treated you disrespectfully – based on your own assessment. They fail to consider your personal needs. They ignored your desire to be heard, and implement their changed ideas at the expense of your own general well-being. You are unhappy about this as your need for pleasure is not met. You have a choice to love. You can love by choosing to forgive their ignorance for failing to consider your needs correctly and be kind to them. This will be a perfect opportunity to demonstrate love. If you could forgive them and treat them with respect and kindness even though they have done the opposite, you will be demonstrating love. This does not mean you are a fool as your decision to love is conscious of humanity's betterment as a whole.

You chose to love as love brings more health, happiness, wealth, and peace for humanity. But what happens if you choose not to love? You can confront them and tell them how badly you have been treated and with that take the path of least resistance to hell. You can give them what they deserve – be unkind to them and do what will ensure they feel the pain of their unkindness. While you conduct your affairs in this way, the secret of life is that your internal cellular structure does the same. The thoughts you hold in mind are passed on through the nervous systems to various organs instructed to start a fight against an attacker. Your stress level goes up as the hormones for fighting this attack signal that an internal war is now on. This negative energy permeates your environment, and if you think about the billions of people doing the same, the wars and eruptions in our ecosystem should be no surprise to you.

Sages knew that for love to be present, the opposite should be in existence. Hence the definition of love covers all transgression. When we do not know what love is, we fight hate with hate and create more hate. Everyone can say I love you to another; however, the acid test is what we do when hate appears.

Humanity is always chasing out hate with fire because we have never truly understood what love is. Love holds the foundation of our existence. If there were no love in nature, we would not have been in existence. Love is giving. Rather than fight hate with hate, give love where hate has been demonstrated. Hate is the ego's sensation that it has not received pleasure. However, love is the soul's sensation that has given pleasure to another.

Do you see how the two forces within are supposed to be used? You have the right to develop your soul – that is the essence of life. You have the ultimate goal through nature to develop your soul, and your ego is the vehicle through which it can be developed. The soul gives, and the ego receives. These are the plus and minus forces that operate in nature and within you. Connecting with others is the means through which you demonstrate love and become whole. The resistance within is the hurdle you must overcome to heal your troubles. Love is for you and not against you. If there is no transgression, meaning the sensation of offence, you cannot demonstrate love.

All the wars, conflicts in relationships, marital breakups, and family disputes are all designed to allow you to love. Love gives life, and without love, death ensues. When you resist love, you prevent life from flowing into this system called nature.

> **"Hate is the ego's sensation that it has not received pleasure. However, love is the soul's sensation that has given pleasure to another."**

Every time you love, you breathe life into the system. The act of prayer for others is a demonstration of love. Praying for yourself is self-centred because your thoughts are towards the self. Praying for others is an act of giving, and giving is love.

Therefore, love is the best medicine for hate. Fighting hate with hate is a recipe for disaster. Hate only grows because it is like saying, you will see to it that others do not get their needs satisfied and in the process of doing so, nature makes sure your own needs are not satisfied. Why? The reason is simple: what you give others, you give yourself first. Nature gives you what you give to others. Therefore, you cannot give hate and receive love. The system does not work this way. Love dissolves hate but hate never dissolves love because love is a higher vibration and will always overpower hate.

The purpose of life is for humanity to master love. Love is the quality of nature, otherwise known as the Creator. Humanity, if left unchecked, will gravitate to more of his ego-self, which will increase destruction.

To close, when we operate in love, we learn to understand what the other person needs to function properly. We discover various layers of their desires as we delve deeper into the relationship. We are prepared to do so to connect correctly to different portions of their lives.

Sara's Response

The analogy that love is a state similar to **single cells in the body working integrally to support the others paints a vivid image of love in action**. I would recommend you watch a video on the anatomy of healthy cells and how different parts operate in synchronicity and harmony to provide the human body with life forces. Without healthy cells working in harmony in our bodies, we will never experience life or health. This paints the picture of love, which is needed for our well-being at all levels. I must confess, I have never perceived love through the eyes of the humanly body. However, I now do. It makes me realise that everything in nature is shown to us in this physical realm through our physical bodies. Yet, we do not take notice of the lessons. Our internal structures are mirrors of Nature in action. As within, so without.

Without love, we will experience many ills, and it is no surprise that all our challenges point to the absence of love.

I cannot help but notice how dire our life situation is without a proper education about love. We can become so fixated on the conditions of our lives, when the conditions are for us to create life for others. We are oblivious to our world's integrality; observe your thoughts when you interact with others. You will soon realise how your mind works and why you do not connect healthily with others. When someone speaks to us, we have many opinions in opposition to others, except for those who are much wiser to put a lead over these oppositional thoughts. We are constantly battling between thoughts that demean and oppose each other. We are constantly trying to win arguments and, worse still, seek self at others' expense.

> **"Love is when we put the needs of others first, recognising the importance of the entire system over ours."**

Looking at my life now, I am glad that I always professed my ignorance about the subject of love. Had I not challenged my limited education on the subject, it would have been impossible to seek redress and come to this point in my life. One thing is certain, until a person learns how to LOVE unconditionally, they will never be able to build good relationships with others. Our environment is where we learn how to relate to one another. If we were brought up with discordant thoughts, frequent disputes and arguments, we are ill-prepared for good relationships with others. Lack of harmony is our mental DNA. When these conflicting thoughts are practised many times round, they become habits of liability in that they will cause us great harm as we progress in life. It is precisely why one should embark on the journey of change. There is no one you and I can change except ourselves. When you change your love consciousness, your entire world will change. No one can bypass the laws of nature. We get what we are, not what we want. If we live by the principles of disharmony, we will reap the benefits of disharmony.

> **"When you change your love consciousness you will change your world for the better."**

Every action we take when interacting with others, and our environment must be weighed on a love's scale to protect ourselves and others from harmful consequences. We cannot be reckless about this as thoughts of love or hate drive our actions. If the latter, we will destroy others and ourselves. For this reason, we need self-discipline. If we fail to weigh our actions on the scale of love for others or not, we will pay the price down the line to bring us in alignment with nature. The sages' wisdom says that we should love others as we love ourselves is key to our success.

After this conversation, I took a journey back to uncover my challenges. I quickly concluded that love is the answer to resolving them. Every area of conflict scrutinised had the mark of unkindness or absence of love. I urge you the reader to take the same journey into your life circumstances to determine your best cause of action to move forward.

If the right connection ceases between bodily cells, we call this condition toxic. When we experience it between people, we call it conflict and chaos. However, every conflict creates toxicity in our environment internally and with that, we experience the world. The solution is for us to end the conflicts, pouring love over them to bring life and healing into our world. Support is needed to strengthen us to do so. The theory must be practicalised. No one is exempt from this. Our prayers for one another are critical. We need the help of God to take us through this journey confidently. I pray that you will find the strength to do all that it takes to pour love over all transgressions.

Use this time to reflect on what you have read so far and agree with some action points to move to the next degree.

Your Personal Reflection Notes

_____

_____

_____

_____

_____

_____

_____

_____

_____

_____

Chapter 8
Author's conclusion and action points

If you are anything like me, you will be baffled or wowed by the contents shared during these conversations. You will feel a sense of perplexion and wondering what is the next step to take to bring order into your life.

I felt the same when the wisdom came together for me, and no doubt left me rehashing my entire life's journey as though it was happening all over again in one quick scoop.

One thing is certain: it is doubtful you would have grasped all the essence of the wisdom imparted in this book with one reading. Do not underestimate the depth of the message conveyed. See each chapter as a vital masterclass you have attended, for which time is needed to think about your own life and how you will organise it going forward.

We all have stories we will share about our lives. This is what brings us together on many fronts. However, whether your story has been the death of a loved one you struggled to relinquish, the pain of a separation or a marital relationship that ended in divorce, childhood abandonment, abuse of many types, it matters not. All were given for a purpose much higher than our perception through the lens of our ego.

The conversation with the sages is loaded with vitality and life-changing counsel like a precious gem. It is prudent for one to revisit each section repeatedly to remind the inner self why we are on this planet. One of my reviewers' response to the manuscript was no surprise to me. The comment was, 'It was a fascinating read and a lot to digest'. No doubt, it is. But I urge caution not to stop at this level if you truly want to be happy and master love in your life.

As someone who was desperate to solve life's problems, I remember when I had the conversation with the sages written on scraps of papers next to my bed top table, like precious diamonds I could not let go of. I wanted to be sure I grasped every piece of advice to save myself time and money on foolish events devoid of any chance of happiness. I remember how I wondered what life would have been for me had I not been privy to know and learn all that was needed for my happiness. Of course, nothing good can come from lamenting the past. I quickly determined that the best I can do is to work on myself and share this information with others looking for earnest counsel on the reasons for their unhappiness and lack of success.

Sure enough, our society has mastered the art of using all sorts of drugs, psychological techniques, and herbs to trick the brain and nervous system to create a state of happiness. While I have no judgement on the merit of these approaches, as they could serve as a quick fix to overcome mental anguish of all sorts, long-term happiness can rarely, if at all, be sustained through these mediums. I know this for a fact as part of my own spiritual journey, I have been challenged in many facets of my life, leaving me with lots of questions and minimal answers from mainstream resources. I have seen close family members and friends who opted for these approaches, often ending up with more negative side effects as they do not address the soul's needs for true happiness in our lifetime.

Similarly, many self-help books could not save me from mental pain in a sustainable manner when I needed a solution. A deeper understanding is essential rather than barely mouthing off affirmations and a positive mental attitude devoid of life's essence. I can now see where some of these approaches as solutions to our happiness fit in the jigsaw puzzle of life. When I was heavily engaged with them, the missing link was the spiritual understanding of why one must continually focus on unity and connection. I can now see that the bedrock of happiness, peace, and joy is the quality of our relationships with others.

The journey into my conversation with the sages brought with it answers to my many questions. I feel grateful I was given access to this information. I feel grateful I have been gifted the capacity to be courageous to exit my familiar mental territory to pursue truth and spiritual understanding for my betterment and those of my progeny.

As I recount, the year I began having conversations with sages and the many hours of learning and reflections, I learnt so much and began to make changes in my life. At the time, I had no desire to write a book, although I had been an author of a business book and publications in 2008. Everything changed when I began thinking about my children, my external families, and the world at large. How would this knowledge change their life? Suppose my own parents had been the privileged recipients, would this have helped me? The answers to these questions reversed my decision, and I started writing again.

Born into a family that desperately needs this wisdom for their happiness and harmony has been the driving force for the knowledge gained in this journey. I wanted to know more to ensure my children work hard to break free from what I consider to be a generational curse. It would be fair to say, our society is suffering from a lack of moral and spiritual excellence in leadership qualities today, which brings with it many ills in our education system. They too can benefit from this book.

Many who knew me as a child will wonder how on earth I grew up to learn so many subject areas given my life trajectory as a child growing up. I want to say that it may seem like a miracle, but nothing is a coincidence or a miracle, as the sages said. I have a strong desire for spirituality since I remembered myself as a child, often dreaming of going to Jerusalem. My mother must have seen this in me as she frequently handed me psalms to read daily before bedtime. I remember too well running from home to seek solace in churches where I would join in prayers and felt at peace with my inner self. For me, the world was chaotic. I trusted the Creator to take control of my life. The only place I knew I could find this at the time was my local churches. However, my understanding of the Creator/God and how to work on spirituality needed serious sprucing.

By the time I became an adult, my career and financial success were insufficient to bring me happiness. I worked hard at them and failed to be happy in all areas of my life as my family relationships were in turmoil with no end to the race. I needed answers to the failing areas. I was never prepared to let go until I found the answers.

I had been baffled about poverty in Africa despite its rich endowment of natural resources that should be sufficient to make the continent a powerhouse. I needed answers to these questions. What was wrong with our black people, and why were they always fighting? What did we need to know? Many church organisations are planted worldwide, but frictions are frequent with many civil wars. I needed answers, and I prayed fervently for help.

I became blessed with an insatiable desire to aim for the best of all things in life and to trust that everything was possible through an invisible power. I never took no for an answer or accepted the dogmas given to the masses under various guises, without scrutiny and questions. The sages have said we need to open our minds and with this, we will know the truth that will set us free.

On a personal front, the biggest challenge in my life was to hold on to a failing relationship for nearly twenty years, in fear of the stigma of divorce for my children and me. This fear haunted me so badly, leaving me with a sick feeling inside my stomach many times. I could not understand that one cannot be unhappy and be spiritual at the same time. Something is wrong. Crying and screaming in my prayers, I wanted an answer to understand how to live life correctly. I concluded I do not know what love is, nor do I trust those around me to teach me what love is. I do not know my life's purpose, nor do I trust those in my community to teach me what I am living for. They were too busy fighting to take notice of my questions.

Now, I know that I knew nothing about what it takes to build strong relationships and how to choose a partner to build a stable home life. I also did not know how my ego can become the worst enemy within and how to manage my life with this strong opposing force. *I did not know everyone battles their ego and yet everyone expects others to act like saints.*

Finally, I knew nothing about how the mind works and the vices of abhorrent negative beliefs and thoughts about others and self. I can now say the void and dissatisfaction I felt were the urges from a higher knowledge to impact something within to align me with nature's laws.

Everyone should know that their problems are an inner war between the forces of good and evil. Everyone should be armed with the tools to attain homeostasis where good and evil coexist but with a greater amount of love. If I had been privy to the conversation with the sages ten years earlier, some of my struggles could have been abated. There have been times I felt ashamed and angry about life's predicaments that I have had to battle with. However, I know better to get over the negative emotion, concluding there is nothing to be ashamed of, as we are here to rediscover and rebuild ourselves. What would be shameful is the unwillingness to make the changes needed to succeed after learning the sages' wisdom.

As the sages said, we are all small people. We do not know the laws of nature because we do not operate in the quality of nature. At the very least, we all do our best with what we know until we know better. Hence, forgiveness is a paramount act that should be practised relentlessly.

When one is gifted with this wisdom, there is no more excuse to continue business as usual. Yes, mistakes will be made, but they will be like a toddler attempting to walk and falling. Mother Nature is a system, and its laws should be practised, or one will forever be in war with the system at their own peril. We need to take a good look inside and begin the process of change needed to meet our desire for happiness. What would be shameful is the lack of desire to make the sea change to attain happiness following the sages' wisdom.

With this conclusion, I believe that unless all of humanity understands their true nature, the purpose of their lives, and how to master kindness, gratitude, and love for all, life on earth will be plagued with suffering. Without an attempt for spiritual and personal transformation, one is more apt for pursuing all sorts of events and wishful thinking that will inevitably lead to dead ends and emotional traumas. I hope you have found this book useful as part of your own spiritual journey.

If you would like to join a community to ask more questions, please email us at info@sarainnerhealing.com or join our community group – The Sages Wisdom

To end, I have only one question to ask – what are you going to do to improve your life to achieve more happiness and love? Are you going to practise more love and connection, more alignment in your soul's purpose, more happiness through wholeness and perfection – what will change?

Unless you identify what areas of your life should be spruced up and change, nothing will change.

REFLECTION TIME

Use this time to reflect on what you have read so far and agree with some action points to move to the next degree.

Finally, the sages' wisdom teaches us that the quality of the connection between us should be focused on every day. We should modify our qualities to be similar to Nature to reveal the fruits of happiness and love every day and every moment.

Nature is the inclusive concept of everyone. If we disregard the quality of the relationship between us, we disregard Nature, which is the source of life. If we create a good relationship between us, we honour Nature and happiness will follow.

Notes:

_____

_____

_____

_____

Other Resources

You can find other resources from us on Amazon

The Ultimate Prayer Journal

The Ultimate Gratitude Journal

52 Weeks Mind Cleansing Journal

The Ultimate Forgiveness Journal

*A Conversation With The Sages –
Everything You Need To Know About Love*

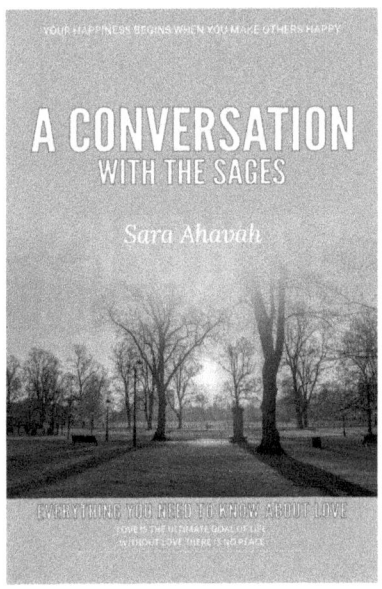

A Conversation With The Sages –
Your Guide To Building Good Relationships

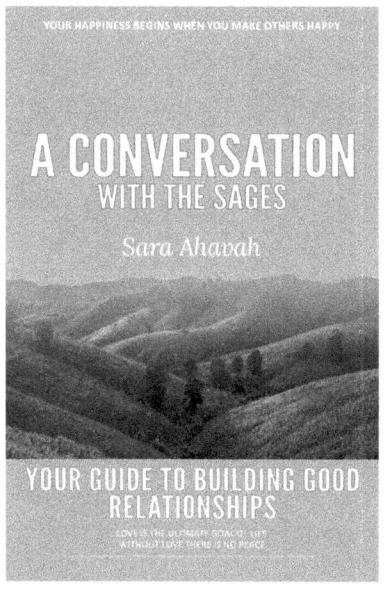

www.ingramcontent.com/pod-product-compliance
Lightning Source LLC
Chambersburg PA
CBHW061326040426
42444CB00011B/2798